The Power of
YOUR IDENTITY

A CULTURAL LANDSCAPE
FOR CHILDREN

The Power of
YOUR IDENTITY

A CULTURAL LANDSCAPE
FOR CHILDREN

Dr. Eunice B. Gwanmesia

Published by Victorious You Press™
Charlotte NC, USA

TITLE: THE POWER OF YOUR IDENTITY
First Printed: 2023

Cover Designer: Nadia Monsano
Editor: Charmaine Castillo

ISBN: 978-1-952756-91-7
ISBN: (eBook) 978-1-952756-92-4
Library of Congress Control Number: 2023900368

Printed in the United States of America

Table of Contents

Dedication

My dear Keith and Kaitlin Gwanmesia,

I wrote this book because of you. I never realized how much our conversations and what we have experienced as a family impacted me as a mother and a diversity, equity, and inclusion strategist. Kaitlin, it warms my heart to see how you express self-awareness and how you show empathy toward others. Thank you, Princess, for always openly sharing your perspective on issues with me even when we do not agree and for reminding me about my core values.

Keith, you are one heck of a dude who sees no limits to what is possible. While others see a disability in you, you only see abilities. As you famously say when you stumble and fall, "I am okay, get up Keith, I can do this" — —you get up and keep going as though nothing happened. Thank you, sweetheart, for teaching me that we should be stronger than the challenges we face.

I pray that one day you will have similar conversations with your children. Someday you will show them a copy of this book and tell them their grandmother was inspired by you to write the book.

Your Lovely Mother,
Eunice. B. Gwanmesia

Foreword – Eric Chinje

Writers and commentators on the evolution of society often have to scour the universe of ideas to identify gaps in our social discourse and in our understanding of the forces that ultimately determine how humans live on this planet. And then they set out to bridge those gaps. The objective is always the same: making the world a better place for those who inhabit it. That is what this book is all about. Dr. Eunice Gwanmesia seeks to address a critical missing element in communal living world-wide and engages us in a rather unique exchange on the fundamental issues of identity, culture, and living together on planet earth.

In this second decade of the 21st century, there are compelling reasons to assess the quality of human relations in a threatened planet. The world today faces existential questions ranging from climate-related devastation, food shortages, uncontrolled inflation to the real possibility of nuclear annihilation. Hunger in the parched lands of Somalia is not unrelated to the war in Ukraine or the value chain disruptions that have resulted in higher cost of living in virtually every country on earth. At the heart of it all is the question of whether we can figure out how to get along; how to deal with matters of cultural identity, diversity, equity, inclusion and that important sense of belonging––issues that constitute the five pillars of this book.

Global headlines and discussions on social media increasingly tend to focus on various expressions of these issues: on immigration and national identity, on the affirmation of individual space and collective identity (think "Black Lives Matter, the #MeToo Movement in the US; IBOP in Nigeria; Ambazonia in Cameroon, etc.); on matters of governance and the quality of leadership in nations and institutions everywhere. There is evident pressure to figure out international laws and regulations that allow people to assert their place in the world and yet allow for mutual co-existence. This book takes a granular approach to dealing with the matter.

The book points to a shrinking global village and the social complexities that come with it, noting that technology, travel, and tourism connect people from different places and cultures at a previously unimaginable scale. Examples in the book illustrate this phenomenon––stories may feature the United States, with characters from other countries and continents. The child from India or Korea who comes to the US with his or her parents will confront a microcosm of the challenges that diplomats at the United Nations or other places of global convergence will have to deal with. This guidebook is for those parents, those children, the teachers and the diplomats.

The book is written in a style that is friendly and accessible to all. It will serve as a traveling companion, a resource for immigrants and receiving communities, a handbook for all parents, and a must-read for children dealing with the crisis of finding a sense of belonging in new environments. It may be just one important response to the toxicity that is becoming the hallmark of our modern social environment in the United States and other parts of the world.

I read the book in one night, but it is a resource I will keep with me and return to every so often. Dr. Gwanmesia gives us more reasons to find a permanent place for it in the office, suitcase, or kitchen––reasons you will discover as you go through this amazingly uncomplicated take on a complex subject.

Acknowledgement

Writing this book was emotionally harder than I thought and more rewarding than I could have ever imagined. This would not have been possible without the support of my awesome family members. I am eternally grateful because none of this would have been possible without your support and encouragement. To my parents, Mary Lamkiyan Manjo and Shey Aloysius WanManjo (RIP) for a solid upbringing and unconditional love and guidance.

The experience of having an idea and turning it into a book can be both internally challenging and rewarding. I want to especially thank my sister and mentor Dr. Linda Arrey Nkwenti, with whom I shared about the idea in its infancy, she immediately went into planning mode and in her usual manner started a conversation about what the book could entail and decreed this book will be on the cover of Essence magazine. Thank you, Sis, for always seeing the possibilities in me and pushing me to live at my full potential. I celebrate you always!

A special thank you goes to the following students, Kylie, Awakinza, Ann Kelly, Kaitlin, and Andrea for taking time out of their busy schedules to share their perspectives on why it is important to know one's cultural identity.

For a special mention are Jevonda Perkins, Helen Ndangam and Tawonga Kwangu Msowoya; your support of this project pushed me to the finish line. I am grateful.

Thanks to everyone on the Victorious You Press Team who helped me so much. Special thanks to Elder. Joan Thaxter-Randall for the prayers and words of encouragement throughout the process of writing this book.

Above all, I want to thank my Lord and Savior for his protection and blessings.

Author's Note

When I was young, I left the cornfields of Cameroon to pursue a higher education in dental therapy in Saskatchewan, Canada. Before this, I had dreams of becoming a teacher like my dad, but at age 21 I had failed out of the University of Yaoundé because I simply couldn't adapt. The experience was difficult, and language was the main barrier I could not overcome at the time.

Dropping out was a turning point for me, and eventually, I made my way to the United States. After my previous difficulties with adapting to a different culture and language, I was determined to succeed this time. More than thirty years later, I've led a career in nursing and education, pursued several degrees, started two businesses, and founded a nonprofit organization.

As an immigrant, mother, caregiver, and educator, I know firsthand the importance of culture, identity, and diversity. I'm incredibly proud and grateful for the opportunities and success I've had. However, many times I felt alone and wished I had guidance, whether it was when I was adjusting to life in a new country, navigating the workplace, raising a child with a disability, or guiding my children through the school system. I've written this book with the hopes of guiding other parents and educators who may be facing similar challenges.

Introduction

Today, our children's education and development have been overshadowed by facts and figures, leaving them feeling stranded about who they really are. Progress and success are measured by standardized tests and numerical grades, and teachers gear curricula to national standards beyond their control. Beyond the classroom, talk of identity, culture, and belonging is often divisive. Young people, Gen Z and Gen A, are growing up against a landscape of deep polarization, and as the first generations to grow up with technology and internet access since early childhood, this landscape is one they're largely unable to escape.

Although too young to remember the culture wars of the 1990s and 9/11 itself, Gen Z and Gen A have seen the fallout from these events, as well as wars and invasions, economic crises, terrorist attacks, natural disasters, and health crises throughout the last two decades. Divisive rhetoric and xenophobia, islamophobia, antisemitism, racism, and far-right nationalism have risen worldwide, and many young people have witnessed such instances firsthand or via news headlines or social media.

With these factors in mind, globalization and its effects may feel bleak. But recent events, globalization, and technology have also been positive. Young people have a wealth of information at their fingertips, allowing them to learn new skills, connect with others worldwide, expose themselves to new ideas and cultures, explore media and creativity, and much more. The world is far more connected, and they're able to travel far more easily than previous generations. And while they've witnessed a host of negatively impactful events, they've also seen historic firsts such as Barack Obama's presidency, the legalization of same-sex marriage, the rise of women's activism through #MeToo and the Women's March, and demonstrations of youth-led activism, whether related to education, the environment, racism, or gun violence.

We and our children are exposed to these crises, events, and phenomena almost constantly through technology and media, and it can be difficult to handle conversations about these topics. Depending on students' age, the school district, and type of school, teachers may cover some of these topics and initiate conversations about current events, culture, and society. This education and secondary socialization are crucial, especially because our children spend a sizeable portion of their lives at school. However, primary socialization—education from family at home—remains important in childhood and adolescent development. Regardless of whether at school or at home, children need guidance to navigate their way through the complex, culturally fluid world we know today.

Fostering dialogue, conversation, and openness is important when educating young people. However, this is often easier said than done. Whether we realize it or not, many of us create walls around ourselves and our children. Perhaps it's because of our own upbringing, or because of our concerns about safety and access to information. Perhaps it's because we don't feel educated enough about certain subjects, or we want to safeguard our family's culture or to assimilate as well as we can. Whatever the reason, sometimes we need our own guidance for navigating the world—and helping our children through it, too.

This book serves as that guide for you. Many of us hope that we raise children who are curious, independent, kind, and understanding. To do that, we must take an active role in implementing open dialogue, creating safe spaces for questions (and even disagreement!), and encouraging listening and understanding. While this book can't cover everything––our world is constantly changing, after all––we will explore concepts such as culture, identity, cultural identity, diversity, equity, inclusion, and belonging. These topics appear frequently as buzzwords in politics and media, so it's valuable for us and our children to have a deeper understanding of them. Several pillars form the structure of this book: cultural identity, diversity, equity, inclusion, and belonging. Within each pillar, or section, there are chapters with discussions and case studies about young people as illustrations for the topic at hand.

Because this book is practical in nature, there are several features included to help you guide dialogue and conversations at home. After reading the book's contents, you'll find a "cultural landscape" of recipes, words, concepts, and a reader's guide. These are designed to complement discussions with your children, and they can also provide a gateway to starting these conversations.

Pillar 1
CULTURAL IDENTITY

A people without knowledge of their past history, origin and culture is like a tree without roots.
- Marcus Garvey

Our exploration of identity begins with a discussion of several key concepts: society, culture, and identity. Our connected, multicultural world means that we're often exposed to unfamiliar cultures, whether through interpersonal interactions, examples in films and TV, travel, media… Understanding our own cultural identities helps us to understand the behaviors and practices of others, and this is a valuable process to guide our children through. These first three chapters provide the foundation for reflection and conversations about our own cultures and the cultures of others.

Chapter 1: Culture and Society

What is society?

Put simply, society is comprised of groups of people or networks that share relationships. But this definition is vague, and we often have varying concepts of what society means. Are these groups of people determined by location or territory, or can a society transcend borders? How big is a society?

A society often shares a geographic space, but more importantly it shares cultures, interests, institutions, patterns of behavior, or infrastructures. We can also categorize society through aspects such as technology and development: anthropologists often discuss preindustrial societies such as hunter gatherer or agrarian groups, or postindustrial society characterized by information and services. Concepts and definitions of "society" may vary depending on context, but the key is that the people in a society share or feel bound together by something in common.

A society, or social group, often adheres to social norms, meaning a set of principles, behaviors, and/or actions that are considered acceptable or unacceptable. These may relate to etiquette, such as greetings and manners, or rituals such as celebrating events or holidays. They include a wide range of behaviors and practices, and they also evolve and change over time. For example, certain social norms exist for using technology––which certainly didn't exist in the past, and in many places, women wear trousers instead of having to adhere to the norm of only wearing skirts and dresses. When talking about society, the idea of social norms is important, as is the wider topic of culture.

What is culture?

Culture generally refers to ways of life, which includes beliefs, traditions, arts, symbols, values, food, and social norms. It can refer to the ways of life of small-scale social groups, such as a specific workplace's culture or a small village's culture, or to those of large-scale social groups, like Islamic culture or internet culture. Many cultures can be defined by geography, class, ethnicity, or other factors, but globalization and the internet have allowed us to expand cultures across borders, and languages.

The concept of culture includes aspects that are both material and non-material, or tangible and intangible. Examples of tangible culture include buildings, monuments, clothing, artifacts, and other physical products. Intangible culture includes practices, knowledge and skills. Material culture appears in the form of machines, clothing, museums, monuments, and religious images. Even entire cities constitute material culture, and many have received protected status from agencies such as UNESCO. The intangible includes religion and spirituality, dancing, weaving, planting and harvesting techniques.

Over time, cultures may change and emerge, and we've all likely seen examples of this in our own lifetimes. As young people, we probably took part in "youth culture" that felt distinct to mainstream culture. We've seen the rise of media culture and the introduction of internet culture, with all its norms and etiquette related to emojis and text abbreviations. Many of us identify with multiple cultures, and our identification with these cultures may change as we age, as well. Values, practices, arts, and traditions can overlap between cultures; in an increasingly connected and multicultural world, it can be valuable and fulfilling to partake and identify with these cultures, while also being challenging from time to time.

How is culture linked to society?

Many of us are quick to tell our kids how we must make efforts to prevent history from repeating itself, but the topic of culture rarely comes up among bookish historical facts. We must remind our children that each of them plays an active role in contributing to the improvement and welfare of civilized society so that they realize its complexities, as well as how culture can influence one's behavior. Teaching children about culture––whether it is the culture of your family, the host culture of a new country, the traditions of other groups––can, and should, balance senses of pride and honor as well as understanding and curiosity. Let us consider a practical example.

> Rachel Kim is a Korean American. In the United States, in general American culture, people do not take off their shoes before entering the house. In Korean culture, wearing your outdoor shoes while inside your own home or in someone else's home is considered disrespectful and unhygienic. Because her parents maintained the same tradition after moving from Korea to

the United States, Rachel picked up this habit while growing up. Now, not only does she do it in her own house, but when she visits her American friends' house, she does it out of habit and a sense of respect as a guest. Even though she was raised in American culture, her family's culture shone through her practices.

Her friends sometimes find it odd, except for those who have learned about the practice or who have backgrounds with similar customs. For example, Burak is a Turkish-American, and his family follows the same custom of removing shoes outside. In Turkish culture, as in Korean culture, people do not bring shoes into the house for hygienic reasons. Despite their different backgrounds and family origins, this simple act gives them a form of common ground.

How does culture affect thinking and behavior?

When speaking of culture, let us take it upon ourselves to shed some light on its different types, material and non-material, each of which can considerably influence thinking processes and behaviors.

Because cultural identity is so influential throughout our lives, it's natural to have feelings about the impact of culture on your life. Some people may feel strongly, while others have little to say about the subject. And while some may view culture as a positive factor and influence, others may have a negative perception of it. Pride, shame, gratitude, ambivalence, acceptance, and denial are all examples of feelings which may be provoked by cultural identity, and we are likely to feel any combination of each of these throughout our lifetime.

Thought processes form a big part of human cognition and generate most of our ideas, mental images, or other imaginary elements that one can experience or manipulate. This ideology generates a universe of problem-solving and concept formation. Since society is an important concept framing human function, it is vital to understand how and why culture affects human thinking and ideology.

When raised in a community that follows certain cultural practices, behaviors, values, and beliefs are often passed down through generations. Many of these things are readily accepted and become second nature, such as Rachel's habit of taking off her shoes before going inside or the American habit of keeping them on. Others may be met with some sort of resistance; your teenager might challenge a traditional gender norm or express distaste for certain foods, for example.

Values passed down generations that originate from a particular culture play the same role. You would feel surprised at how eccentric some of these values may sound. Have you ever heard of sumo wrestlers making babies cry? Yes, you heard that right! The Crying Baby Festival is one of the most prized festivals in Tokyo, Japan. The event hires professional sumo wrestlers who get paid for dangling babies upside down and jiggling them about to see who cries or laughs first. The Japanese believe that this cultural practice helps in warding off evil. What might seem even bizarre to you is that referees accompany the celebration and wear scary-looking masks to egg on the babies to cry more because their tradition makes them believe that crying babies grow healthier.

Because cultures and societies change over time, some traditional cultural practices may no longer take place (or very infrequently). For instance, the foot binding concept in ancient China bound women's feet tightly using cloth strips with the toes bent below the foot sole. Women and men alike received social conditioning that made them believe this practice was beautiful because of the exaggerated curvature of the foot formed due to the binding. However, the practice enforced a gender hierarchy because it made women appear more vulnerable and be vulnerable due to limited mobility.

We can inform our children about cultural identity by engaging in certain practices or traditions at home or in the community. For example, we can celebrate holidays associated with our family's culture, prepare regional foods, dress in certain clothing, attend religious services within the community, and much more. In addition to our active efforts to preserve and teach about culture, our children will be affected by factors much larger than our influences, and it is beneficial for us to consider these factors and teach our children about them as well.

One such factor is the collectivist vs. individualist mindset (Hofstede, 1984)[1]. Certain societies have a far deeper sense of collectivism, community, and relation to others, whereas other societies have a deeper sense of individualism and independence. We can see examples of this

---

[1] For further reading on this subject, see Geert Hofstede, a Dutch social psychologist, developed a framework for understanding differences in culture. Individualism–collectivism was a key dimension.

in South Asian countries, which tend to put greater emphasis on families and communities, group loyalty, and unity. The United States is more individualist and prioritizes uniqueness, self-reliance, and individual rights. These large-scale cultural mindsets affect the way individuals act and behave.

Communicating the significance of cultural identity

Often, we don't even realize the effect that our culture has had on our life. If we notice difference, we may even dismiss or disparage it without much thought. Because we constantly navigate our own cultural identity and can never have a full, true understanding of others' cultural identities, being open to dialogue about the subject is useful and can be thought-provoking.

Maybe your culture values large gatherings of family and friends, and these occasions often run late into the night and are full of laughter, music, and chatting. Neighbors may perceive your late-night noise as rude or inconsiderate. On the other hand, you perceive their behavior as cold and unfriendly rather than as a reflection of their values of privacy, personal space, and calmness. This difference, of course, is unlikely to be resolved by either party

25

sacrificing something they hold so close to their heart. Perhaps neither party thinks there is a problem worth solving, or that there's no way to approach it even if they wanted to. And while there may not be an easy path for communication, it could begin with an act as simple as inviting the neighbors to join the next celebration, maybe noting that you love to be surrounded by family and friends on such occasions. Maybe the neighbor joins in and leaves the evening with a different perspective on noise and rudeness, or maybe they decline but offer a one-on-one afternoon teatime to get to know one another better.

Regardless of the situation and context–and whether it feels like a celebration of or a clash of cultures, whatever scale–communicating about culture and its impact on your life requires vulnerability, openness, and courage.

Cultural identity formation

With these factors (society, social norms, culture, and identity) in mind, we can think more deeply about the way identity forms. It's useful to reflect upon your own cultural identity, perhaps identifying cultural groups you feel a connection with, cultural practices you partake in, and differences you may have noticed between your culture and others. These thought processes can guide you through traditions with your family as well as conversations with your children about these topics.

When considering the formation of the cultural identity, it can be helpful to frame its evolution within three stages. Reflecting on our own journey through this formation is a valuable practice; it encourages self-reflection and can help you understand and empathize with others in the stages you have experienced. The first stage is one in which cultural identity is unexamined. At this point, there may be little interest in cultural interests, often because personal cultural characteristics are simply assumed, not questioned, or rarely dwelled upon. The second stage involves general exploration of our culture with the intention to discover more about it. This might manifest as an interest in certain cultural practices, a desire to research culture and heritage, and connecting with others from the particular culture. The third stage solidifies, to an extent, that culture. Although, as this book discusses, cultural identity can change and evolve over time, this stage remains relevant. It is the time that we accept ourselves and internalize the cultural identity that we've explored and decided resonates with us.

Personal, social, and cultural identities

When we think about who we are, a variety of factors come to mind that may include concepts such as: physical appearance (I'm tall and brunette); personality traits (I'm outgoing); group membership (I'm a Muslim); family role (I'm a father and husband); or profession (I'm a teacher). Our self-concept reflects a multitude of descriptors and experiences, and this self-concept changes over time.

Identity is often categorized into three groups. Our personal identities are those that are largely personal and related to our individual life experiences, such as being someone who loves to read or someone who loves to play the guitar. Social identities derive from social groups we take part in, whether that membership is voluntary or involuntary, or explicit or implicit. These identities are usually externally organized, such as being a member of the humane society (voluntary, explicit), or being a member of your family (involuntary). Cultural identities are related to socially constructed categories, and we typically have them from birth and throughout life. They are often the least likely to change over time. Examples include nationality, gender, race, or sexuality.

We can choose certain aspects of our identity, or whether to identify with or claim them. But other aspects of our identity may be placed upon us by others, often based on stereotypes. Sometimes, these identities do not match up, and this can be a confusing experience. From birth, we've experienced the formation of our identity and seen personal, social, and cultural factors. Helping your child understand their own identity can provide them a better sense of self and more self-confidence.

Now you must be wondering how identity and culture get considered so closely knit together that people often mistake them for being the same or holding equal weight. When we talk about seeing through the culture to define what it should mean to our children, we essentially tell them what should become acceptable to them. Hence, we are creating their sense of self in their early stages of socialization. Such a sense of self is bound to face change, just like it is applied to cultural practices because our children come across all sorts of experiences, relationships, and memories that make them think a certain way. But when asked who we are or what we think of ourselves, we often feel stumped, as though there exists no one answer to this question.

The reason for this could be that in our routine lives we switch between all sorts of roles within professional and individual life and accepting that it's only human to sometimes feel all over the place is the first step towards acceptance and progress. A woman who is a daughter today might be a mother tomorrow, or perhaps a lawyer or a teacher. When shifting between acquired gender roles, a person might go through a shift in relationship dynamics which can affect their sense of self. External factors have their part to play in matters such as these, for instance: your height, skin color, race, socio economic and religious background, or cultural and social orientation.

Family and identity

Making sense of identity can feel tricky and even leave us isolated and uncertain. Perhaps when we pile things under the rug and stop our intellect from expanding or when we try to over-influence our kids with our ways, we sow the seed for destruction. Having conversations with our children about our identities and their own identities can be productive and beneficial, as well as lead them to be more understanding of others.

We often feel helpless when we feel pressured by people labeling us a certain way, leading to the birth of ascribed identities—the identities others project onto us. These often consist of stereotypes and can be difficult to avoid. For instance, a boy from Asia enrolled in an American school may be presumed to have good mathematical skills, even if he does not, because a common stereotype is Asian people being math whizzes. While stereotypes may sometimes have an element of truth to them, such labeling often does more harm than good; making assumptions or holding others to unrealistic expectations can dangerously affect someone's self-perception and behavior.

However, some children adopt acceptance as an effective defense mechanism where they make it a point to live up to their labels and take pride in them, and the idea has even led to the existence of nerd culture. We must encourage our children to continue reading books and keeping themselves well-informed about world affairs because it is their field of interest despite being labeled as "nerdy" by their friends. It should be considered nothing short of a victory for us adults, and we must learn to celebrate this small victory for them. However, if we reinforce those same labels at home, we are no better than the children who say whatever comes to mind in the heat of adolescence. And we must do better and try harder with our kids because their futures start with us.

Properties of cultural identity

Because our identities are influenced by personal and external factors, there are different properties to consider when thinking about cultural identity. An individual's cultural identity can either be based upon their perception of themselves or based upon others' perceptions of them. The way in which someone perceives and expresses their identity is "avowal," and the way others perceive and communicate that person's identity is "ascription."

Case studies: construction and representation of cultural identity

When a group of Turkish students were asked how they would categorize themselves in a diverse setting, their answers revealed insights about dynamics between those from the dominant culture and those from marginalized cultures (Güneri, Sümer, & Yildirim, 1999).

Most emphasized their religious and ethnic backgrounds, and many prioritized their Muslim identity over their Turkish or Kurd ethnicity. Some felt that describing themselves as Turkish automatically indicates being Muslim. Since their identification strongly relied on institutionalized religion, nation-state formation, and ethnic belonging, it was clear that identity formation had to do with ethnic belongingness. Those who described their religion and their ethnic origin demonstrated signs of clear identity formation. Other answers indicated less certainty or confidence, which could represent the difficulty of choosing simple descriptors or membership to particular groups to describe what might be a complex, multifaceted identity.

Identity can cause a sense of conflict or confusion for individuals, but we also constantly see how identity can cause interpersonal and intergroup conflict. From the students in Turkey, this could be seen among those who shared a religion but had different ethnicities. Despite a shared ideology and belief, their feelings of belonging to different groups can cause rifts that pull them apart.

In this study, a Kurdish student expressed disgust towards his Turkish friends when they bullied him in the name of cultural identity and then bragged about their badges and cultural heritage to symbolize the Turkish flag. He explained how several of his friends displayed political symbols inked onto their skins as if heritage mattered more to them than the blood. Such division can have damaging consequences on a person-to-person level, especially at formative ages.

It is interesting to see how dominant culture plays out in a setting where several cultures are at threat of being 'marginalized'. Those who are "authorized" by the dominant groups fall victim to being misunderstood when they try fighting off implementations, often being labeled as "divider" and "separatist." However, the *othering* process could cause more harm and spread beyond the extent of the family and education/workplace leading to social issues like political turmoil, ethnic cleansing, terror, and even civil wars. Our own lifetimes have witnessed how violent conflict can manifest when this rhetoric is translated into a larger scale, between groups or nations.

In a place like Turkey, extremist nationalist movements are on the rise with slowly emerging various ethnic groups, provided that the role played by the state is that of a mediator. When deep-rooted identities take hold, and when politicians capitalize on this with propaganda and further divisive rhetoric, it becomes difficult to combat hate.

It is our responsibility to social and cultural awareness in our children as they navigate the diverse world around them. Although individual efforts as parents, teachers, and role models may feel insignificant in comparison to the conflict and division around us, we have the opportunity to foster the understanding and empathy necessary to resist the power of division. The story of James is an illustration of how identity, even when different from others, can contribute to relationship building and deeper self-understanding.

> James Raj was born in India and moved to the United States as a child. All his life, he had lived with people following either Christianity (like himself), Islam, or Hinduism. He noticed a connection between the three religions—the end goal may be different, but religion still played a prominent role in people's lives, and it did not seem like people wished to exist without a purpose.
>
> Later in life, he encountered several groups of atheists in the USA, and his connection to such groups, despite provoking an initial cultural shock, evolved into a relationship of appreciation. He found it fascinating how

they boldly admitted they were not searching for an end purpose to life and they were comfortable in their skins not believing in anything. That they required no set religiously driven morals for governing their lives and nor did they feel to attach logic to their actions.

Stories like James's as well as the examples above from groups in Turkey provide interesting examples of identity formation and the influence that our own identity has on the way we interact with others.

We can conclude that constructing your own identity amongst a group of ethnically and culturally diverse people is important to have a sense of self, as well as connections to and understanding of family, community, and heritage. Doing so, however, must not come at the expense of others' identities or dignity. Discussing differences and diversity should be used to cultivate learning and understanding, not as a tool for *othering* and marginalizing.

One of the many takeaways of the chapter is that being comfortable in your own skin can help you gain a better outcome when interacting with people from different cultures to our own. New situations of all kinds can induce uncertainty, but interactions with unfamiliar cultures or traditions should be embraced. At times, of course, we—

and our children—may encounter awkward situations or moments that feel uncomfortable. But this type of discomfort can often teach us valuable insights about ourselves when we take the time to sit with the feeling. It can help lay the groundwork for analyzing the interactions our kids experience daily to help us understand them better and aid us to become better parents. Approaching intercultural exchanges or interactions with people who are different from us is also a productive and meaningful way to serve as a role model for children.

Key reflections

- o "Culture" generally refers to ways of life, which includes beliefs, traditions, arts, symbols, values, food, social norms, etc. It can refer to the ways of life of small-scale social groups, such as a specific workplace culture or a small village's culture, or to those of large-scale social groups,

- o We can choose certain aspects of our identity, or whether to identify with or claim them. But other aspects of our identity may be placed upon us by others, often based on stereotypes.

- o Identity is normally categorized into three categories: personal, social, cultural.

- o Discussing differences and diversity should be used to cultivate learning and understanding, not as a tool for *othering* and marginalizing.

Chapter 2: Power of Cultural Identity

What is cultural identity?

As discussed in the previous chapter, there are a variety of factors that influence cultural identity. Regardless of where or how you were raised, it is likely that you took part in some sort of community that follows certain cultural practices, behaviors, values, and beliefs that are often passed down through generations. Cultural identity is typically introduced during our upbringing, but it is malleable and might change throughout your lifetime, particularly if you become involved in a new community, for example a new religion, or move to an area that differs greatly from the one in which you grew up.

As a parent or teacher, you can introduce and pass on aspects of cultural identity––sometimes without even realizing! ––by incorporating traditions, cooking, listening to music, interacting with different art forms, or following religious practices.

Cultural identity and discomfort

How many of us growing up wished our mums took it easy on us? How desperately did we want to get called *the cool kids*? How frustrating was it when a phone call from the parents always disrupted you? That is the way of the world that you only ever realize the intensity or the reasoning behind something when you get a dose of the experience itself.

Then what do you do when it is time to pack your child's first lunch and when you find yourself trimming the hem of your daughter's school uniform to ensure she has the perfect first day? You always knew the time would fly, but little did you plan on what you would do once it did. What do you do now? Prepare a shell to encapsulate your children forever. But you know perfectly well it will break before you know it because even a bird takes flight and leaves its nest when it grows its wings.

Are you scared of the raised eyebrows or the frowned looks your child might receive on their first day of school? Do you fear the knots of your daughter's Ghana braids are as tightly woven as the knots of deep-rooted negligence and oppression in today's hostile world? Or are the double-lidded eyelids of your Asian son in American society becoming a cause of your concern?

So where do you channel this fear and hesitancy? Is it the uncertainty of the future that makes you queasy, or is it the certainty that society would not accept the new face of culture your child brings to the table? Getting comfortable with discomfort is easier said than done, but it is a valuable thing to attempt, and it becomes easier over time.

Why does cultural identity matter?

Having a sense of cultural identity can provide a feeling of connection to oneself, family, friends, and larger communities. Feeling connected and understood prevents loneliness and isolation. And when living with one cultural identity and encountering others, having a sense of self and an understanding of personal cultural identity can allow openness and understanding of others, too. It may seem slightly counterintuitive, but imagine, for example, that a British child with a connection to Christianity meets a Lebanese child with a connection to Islam. As children, we can assume they wouldn't begin discussions about cultural and religious identities out of the blue. But although their cultural and religious identities may differ, the British child may be able to better understand Islamic religious holidays and traditions and their significance when they understand their own religious traditions, and vice versa.

Cultural identity: a teacher-parent perspective

Questions like these can take up several faces, but one of the ways we can ever counter this hostility is when we examine deeper insights into what exactly goes into the system that stems from the seed of uneasiness. For this reason, parental and teacher perspectives hold significant value. As humans, we sometimes forget how strong of an effect words can have on the receiver, which is a mistake we make as mentors, especially when taking up the role of either the parent or teacher, both equally important in the cultural development of the child.

One of the many reasons the school goes several steps ahead of the indoctrination of cultural values, as seen in the family, is that it develops a sense of social solidarity. It results in a broadening of minds where the child perceives society as larger than him. When the child begins to see how real, powerful, and alive society is, he starts to develop a sense of commitment and belonging to it, a sense of giving back (Durkheim, 1956).

For instance, in an American education curriculum, a child with Hispanic or Asian heritage gets to learn about norms and values, including history only central to the US, which is how he develops a sense of allegiance to American historical systems, and that integrates him into the society he grows in. This type of socialization is very different from the ones observed with family and kin, the former based on kinship relationships and the latter based on free will and choice. Hence, this third variety creates a realization that they must learn to interact with people they might not agree with or share the same values inside a social system defined by socially integrated rules of conduct and behavior. According to Durkheim, it is the first step for the child towards respecting the notions of this world (Durkheim, 1956).

Research suggests that the individual now moves on to the more universalistic standards of understanding himself, shifted to achieved status, unlike the previous ascribed status he received within a family framework. In short, the timeline followed by the educational sector in an industrial family starts from the instilling of society's norms and values for preparing the youth to take up adult roles, selecting and assorting the youth based on their skills and talent, and then prepping them to execute those roles in their adult lives.

Classroom interactions and cultural identities

Since classroom interactions always involve the presence of a teacher, we can safely claim that they play an essential role in creating a self-image for the students. For instance, if teachers give a sense of emotional security for opening up to diversity, the kids will grow up to accept it as the right way to go. Kids are heavily influenced by their teachers because of how sensitive they are to the wordings and attributes the teachers give to every student, and their inquisitive minds make them extra. The social value and presence of the students strongly rely on the teacher's response, which is the foundation of a strong teacher-student interaction (Hughes, Cavell, & Wilson, 2001).

The reason for understanding the classroom dynamic is for the teachers who are reading this to realize their power and how easily they can steer this power in the right direction. A teacher can generate positive connotations and help cancel out negative stereotyping by showing positive affirmations to those kids, especially those who come from ethnic minorities and are already expecting to get bullied. Second, positive role modeling involves a set of orientations and standard norms which strengthen student-teacher relationships. When the students observe the same treatment given to kids from socioeconomic backgrounds, they make it a point to implement the same, leading to a fall in ethnic discrimination (Benner & Graham, 2013).

In a case where a student gets bullied for any reason, and the bully gets called out by the teacher, it signals to the other kids that the classroom is a safe, no judgment zone. In this way, universal emotional support and motivation can help eliminate class hierarchies and increase chances for social acceptance. Positive relations, such as acceptance and respect, develop and replace room for social aggression and acceptance, which leads to healthy social development.

Third, when teachers show emotional support, the students learn to confide and feel secure in taking emotional risks with their peers. Since kids already develop social hierarchies by the time they graduate from preschool, they learn to stay on their guard during cross-ethnic interactions. When the kids interact with peers from diverse ethnicities, they might face a negative peer experience now and then, but with the emotional security provided, such interactions seem natural and promote positive expectations nonetheless (Thijs, 2017).

Negative stereotypes in the classroom

An example to demonstrate how negative teacher-student interactions can sometimes go, a famous sociologist, Cecile Wright, conducted an ethnographic study (Wright, 1992). The study performed on four inner city primary schools displayed the teacher labeling theory of ethnic minority students, which made it harder for such students to gel with the native American kids.

Results from the study showed that Asian students often get ignored and excluded from classroom discussions because of their weaker hold over the English language. And what is even weirder is that whenever the teachers did interact with them, they deliberately "dumbed down" their vocabulary, thinking that it would make it easier for them to interact with the children. But it only creates stronger insecurity for the kids, and they begin to label themselves and set their ethnicity apart from the others. It instigates nothing but a concept of *me vs. them.*

A lack of awareness of cultural values often left the teachers doing what the kids' parents feared most when sending them to an inter-ethnic school. Since Asian girls are culturally expected to remain quiet, almost meek, and submissive to look more "feminine" and "likable", the teachers hardly noticed them inside the classroom. Girls who wished to have more privacy during sports period got looked down on and were hindered from it by their instructors. Such ideas reinstated cultural insensitivity and signaled to the kids that they must mold their personalities and values to the dominant culture if they wished to survive within it.

Perhaps most people with South Asian backgrounds can relate to having strict parents and deadlines for coming back home at the given time. Part of it pertained to safety, but the other was purely cultural. However, what we do not wish for, is getting reminded at school of the same problems we witness at home. For many kids from an ethnic minority country, it already feels hard enough to bear with strict parents in a place where their peers do not have to deal with the same problems. Immigration and globalization already leave them stranded and looking for ways to assimilate into the host culture, and matters get made worse when the same ideology gets imposed on them with gender stereotyping at school.

One of the many stereotypical comments witnessed included the teachers debating whether it would be worth it for them to hand over the permission letters for an overnight field trip to the Asian students because the odds were that they would not be allowed to come to it. Such behaviors only encourage the other students to classify the Asians as "different" and "backward" in relation to themselves, making them feel isolated, and wishing they could escape their ethnic roots.

Such patterns further caused an abandonment of Asian cultural values and beliefs. Even at Asian festivals, the students hardly demonstrated any pride in their backgrounds since they assumed doing the opposite of it would instigate further harassment and judgment by their American counterparts. However, on the plus side, positive labeling of the teachers toward the Asian students with their expectations that the kids would do well academically helped them do better at school. But this is an exaggerated generalization of all members of the social group and can cause the kids to face more academic stress to meet such unrealistic expectations.

Black Caribbean students received their share of cultural injustice as they were expected to be more "unruly" and "rowdy" than the other kids. They were often quick in punishing their frequent episodes of 'misconduct' and chose to stay oblivious that the kids would have faced some levels of racism at some point in their lives. For instance, Marcus got scolded for blurting out the correct answers while the white students received no such treatment. Even though the white students were more likely to be punished outside the class, sent for a visit to the head teacher, or have their privileges terminated, the Caribbean students still received an unfair amount of displeasure from the teachers.

Since the teacher often mispronounced the names of the kids from minority ethnic cultures, it caused the white kids to look down on them, making their culture appear exotic, difficult, or unimportant. Differentiating the white students from the rest also opened pathways for racism amongst the students. In some instances, the white children often refused to include the Asian children in their play and sometimes even made use of threatening slogans, aggression, and physical assault.

The study concludes by suggesting that sometimes it is not the teachers running the system to blame since they do try to promote multiculturalism and equality, but it mostly goes off track because of poor execution and planning. Such negligence towards the kids had some very serious and permanent effects on the ways they come to view the world and the opinion they form over their educational experiences. Perhaps the first step in making education more decentralized around the host culture is to shift its focus from the teacher to the student. A conscious effort to understand the student's personality, needs, learning habits, and mannerisms associated with their culture can go a long way in developing a strong student-teacher rapport.

Introducing modern ways of education for the students, which brings them outside of the classroom setting, might not be a permanent solution because it involves running away from the problem rather than towards it. However, it might open doors for the kids to learn behind the safety shield of a screen and make teaching more vivid and flexible. If the students, such as the Asian girls mentioned above, feel too shy for in-person interaction with their teachers, then they can communicate via the internet.

Loss of cultural identity

At times, cultural identity may become lost, weakened, or even denied. This could happen for a variety of reasons. Perhaps, for example, peers mock or make fun of traditional cultural clothing or of "foreign" or "ethnic" food. In response, the clothing or food may be left at home next time in favor of options that are not so obviously different. Self-consciousness and shame can lead someone to suppress such aspects of their cultural identity in order to avoid shame and to gain more acceptance from those around them.

Loss of cultural identity may not be intentional, though. As time progresses and generations change, ancestors and elders may no longer be around to provide examples of or knowledge of customs and traditions. Certain traditions might even be neglected, such as traditional crafts and arts, as modern technology and machinery provide more efficient or automated processes. With developments like this, knowledge and cultural identity can be neglected or forgotten over time.

Preventing loss of cultural identity

Rigorous attempts by the teachers to give special attention and additional time to the students adjusting to a new curriculum (which is very different from the curriculum they have been accustomed to) can help fix relations with their students. It can build better learning by building a strong footing of some of the basic skills, which helps in strengthening their knowledge reserve. A change in the curriculum can help preserve cultural diversity by transmitting key concepts centralized around intellectual diversity to understand cross cultures and promote social progress.

Perhaps now is the best time for me to ask you this question. Consider it a takeaway message from the chapter, a connection that can prove useful to most of you for your daily interactions. Do you think personality and culture fall under the same category, or that one relies on the other? How often do we think of extracting the deepest, darkest roots of a particular culture only to understand the layers of personality that it gives birth to?

An observation by Ralph Linton would tell you how there exists a need, almost a hunger for human beings to "accumulate their knowledge of all that goes into a set of cultural values, and how useful studying and forming presuppositions based on these can be in understanding personalities" (Linton, 2013). A takeaway message for the teachers reading this is to use the power of knowledge, research, and open communication in developing empathy for their students and to develop newly found respect for the students of marginalized groups.

Since globalization has led to the fear of losing cultural heritage, people have now started to learn the importance of their grassroots, and a "cultural fever" seems to rise out of it. Matters such as cultural heritage receive special attention in places such as China, where the National Museum has held exhibitions to preserve its "crude" and most "ecological version" of their ethnic heritage.

Lastly, and this goes for anyone faced with a near culture crisis, a balance between cultural experiences can help create self-awareness and help you find a way to deal with a clash of multiple identities. While being flexible is the best way to go, we must stay connected to our roots. Suppose you like playing basketball with your American friends but going to your parents on the way back to cook them a meal could be good for you. Sometimes we need to accept the fact that when you introduce yourself to a new way of life, experiences can make you attach negative feelings, but we must try to look for the good in the new culture we wish to immerse ourselves in, and we must learn to appreciate it so that we can take the two cultures together.

Remember, that kids are mirrors of ourselves, so what better way to influence them than to give them the best, most positive role modeling? You would be surprised at how they sometimes only need good reminders. That it is not their fault to want to stay fluid, be it their sexuality or identity, or that it is vital to celebrate how they are from the inside as much as their appearances on the outside. Or that their mannerisms and emotional intelligence frame who they are, not the cultural values attached to them, even though those can get used to forming a positive way forward. Helping our kids find the beauty and joy they wish to see in the world starts off with being more compassionate towards them and developing cordial relations with them, because how we set the roles in the house affects their cultural values.

Key reflections

- o Cultural identity is typically introduced during our upbringing, but it is malleable and might change throughout your lifetime.

- o Having a sense of cultural identity can provide a feeling of connection to oneself, family, friends, and larger communities.

- o Use the power of knowledge, research, and open communication in developing empathy for children and to develop respect for those in marginalized groups.

- o Children are mirrors of us, so you can positively influence them by giving them the best, most positive role modeling.

Chapter 3: Case Study

Perhaps an appreciation of diverse cultures to preserve your origins can help fight a cultural crisis in the long run. But what do we understand by it? Do we rank it as the last straw when the clash of societies causes us to lose track of who we are as individuals? Judging by such a definition, would you perhaps describe the sociocultural crisis as a process of de-identification, or rather, a loss of safety? It brings us to the conclusion that we can essentially define a cultural crisis as a dysfunction in the dynamics or form of a given culture.

When we define someone faced with a cultural crisis, we talk about how they no longer wish to associate themselves with a particular culture. Conflicts between different cultural groups make it difficult for human cultural kinship. Common ground for each culture, which can be instrumental in bringing them together, no longer exists and no longer proves effective. It leads to a transition phase from one way of life into another but gives little indication of the course this action would take up. Perhaps concepts best get understood when we back them up using practical examples. Let us take the example of Sarah, a 16-year-old student who attends a high school in Florida.

Case study

> At Sarah's school, most students come from a Hispanic background. The twist in the story, however, comes from Sarah telling everyone that she is Dominican even though her mom is Jamaican and her dad Indian. Since both Sarah's hair and skin tone suit the ethnicity, she tries to project it makes it easier for her to play along with the facade, and the cherry on top is that she can speak Spanish fluently. We can say that she was biracial, but there was no trace of Hispanic heritage as she had boldly claimed. However, she later marries a Hispanic man, which further is evidence of her will to be associated with the culture she projects.

Question: Why did the character see the need to fit into a culture that was not hers or change her identity?

Now you would probably find yourself thinking, "Why on Earth someone would go to this extent to hide their personality?" There is great ambiguity in whether the whole facade was triggered due to her past experiences or if it was only a safe way out. Or if her purpose was to escape her identity to fit into any other and run away from her own, or whether she chose to culturally assimilate into the Hispanic lifestyle only because her peers shared the same values.

While cultural crises and a loss of cultural values can be easy to explain in terms of a generic definition, understanding why it exists can become a challenging conclusion, especially when studying a particular individual. Being mothers and teachers, we already know how complex the human mind can sometimes get and how difficult it can be to get into the inside of it to understand how human cognition works.

The cultural add vs. cultural fit theory can help us grasp this better because it compares the two mindsets together and shows what happens when someone feels all over the place with their own identity.

Question: Why did Sarah identify with being from the Dominican Republic instead of Jamaica or India?

Another interesting question is why Sarah expressed an affinity for the Dominican Republic rather than Jamaica or India, given her own background. In a setting where she is surrounded by a fairly homogenous group, she would be clearly differentiating herself from the majority if she chose to embrace and outwardly project aspects of her Jamaican or Indian heritage. Young people often struggle with feelings of belonging and acceptance by peers, so perhaps Sarah found it more comfortable to suppress her own heritage and avoid drawing attention to herself and her cultural differences. Given her Spanish fluency, physical appearance, and presence in a Hispanic-majority student body, it is also possible that others simply made assumptions about her ethnicity and background, and she agreed with these assumptions and adopted them as her identity.

Regardless of the exact thought process she had, (which would likely not be logically sound from an adult perspective, even if it made sense to her in some way), we can guess that she had a strong desire to fit in with her peers. But sacrificing aspects of her background, especially in such a clearly misleading way, neglects her upbringing and cultural background. Perhaps if she felt more comfortable in her Jamaican and Indian heritage, or if she felt less threat of ostracism from her peers, she would not have claimed a false cultural identity.

"Cultural add" vs. "cultural fit"

Cultural add and cultural fit describe reactions to changing a cultural identity. Cultural add can be considered the act of embracing cultural traditions and heritage, actively incorporating them within lifestyle and identity, whereas cultural fit leans towards reducing perceived difference with the aim to fit in more with the dominant, mainstream, or host culture and identity. Cultural add takes a more radical approach to reforming or changing the cultural values one originates from, or to fill any voids they feel exist in their traditions. However, those who feel scared to leap and want to play it safe adopt more of the culture fit mindset, where they try to work around the already existing elements and retain them. Where one favors diversity and innovation, seeking the good from a magnitude of cultures and sewing them together, the other calls for an almost stagnant, monotonous continuation and indoctrination of the same norms and values.

About this case study, it is clear that Sarah wishes to follow a more culture-fit mindset, except that it has more to do with a culture she is not connected to by blood. The change in setting puts off the dynamic of the theory a bit but we must remember understanding culture can never be as black and white as it might appear on Google search engines, and the beauty of it lies in the multiple gray areas we mostly pay a deaf ear and a blind eye to.

Then how do we draw conclusions for the study, and what factors do we cash in to explain Sarah's choice? Could it be her hair, accent, or the language she tries to hide, and at the same time, use some of the same elements to her advantage to hide her place of origin? It is obvious from the case study that Sarah's hair on features never was a problem for her in the sense that these were firstly factors that she hardly had any control over, and secondly because they fit in perfectly with the hidden identity she was trying to live with.

An interesting phenomenon that has gained attention on social media in recent years is *black fishing* (Stevens, 2021). This concept is a play on "catfishing," or the act of willfully deceiving others about their appearance and/or identity, typically online or on dating platforms. Black fishing refers specifically to non-Black people imitating characteristics, mannerisms, speech patterns and vocabulary, aspects of physical appearance, and other traits associated with Black culture in the USA. This may manifest as girls deepening the color of their skin through excessive tanning or fake tanning methods, wearing their hair in styles typically worn by Black women, adopting African American Vernacular English (AAVE), or otherwise altering their whiteness in favor of projecting a different identity.

When called out, some may strongly defend their choices and deny ever intentionally misleading others. Some may even claim that their choices indicate an appreciation for Black culture. Regardless of their response, the phenomenon is an interesting one, particularly when someone from a privileged group makes a choice to claim the identity of a marginalized group. Since black fishing appears frequently on social media platforms, the subject could be a relevant starting point for your people about the topic of identity.

Other studies like the one by Prudence Carter, a current professor at Stanford University, suggest that the 70 low-income black and Latino students at the school were not trying to deliberately do poorly in school to prevent looking or acting white (Carter, 2006). What they actually wanted to avoid was the deeply rooted peer culture that prevented them from establishing cordial relations with the teachers and school community.

From such studies, we can conclude that Sarah's attempts to hide where she came from had to do with avoiding hostile peer interactions to fit in well with the kids and avoid any trouble. The 'How dare you?' attitude of the kids when someone comments on their clothing or accent shows how they face people who outlaw and denigrate their identity to the point that they become disillusioned and defiant about it. Sometimes such connotations might not have to do with the person's cultural identity, but they still choose to take it personally because that is what they will nevertheless assume it to be. However, Carter says that some children were good at balancing the two cultures together in that they were popular with children from both black and white backgrounds and still did well at school. She suggests that despite all the ethnic tension, such kids must be appreciated more and considered models for the other students because of how difficult it is not to feel faced with an identity crisis in such an environment (Carter, 2006).

Cross-cultural interactions and making sense of them

However, some kids might be good with the other kids while still being good at studies and successfully hiding their identities, and Sarah could be considered an ideal example of this. It could be possible that there still existed elements in Sarah's Indian culture she appreciated and did not consider to be all bad as might seem when we first read her case. Most Indian students, when exposed to American or Spanish today, come to appreciate some of the restrictions that exist within their society. They may find it hard, and sometimes even impossible, to accept the fluidity surrounding emotional connections and interactions within people.

Young people like Sarah, who transition through different stages in their teenage life and come to see the world differently, can be fickle in their opinions. Perhaps Sarah felt her father's Indian heritage was more traditional than the way she wanted to live, in terms of expectations of marriage, career, etc. She may have felt similarly about her

Jamaican heritage. Negative associations from home with either or both may have made her reluctant to embrace them, or she may have witnessed or experienced discrimination due to those identities and decided to suppress them to avoid similar situations.

Maybe this changes when she grows up to realize the advantages of being bilingual or of preserving your cultural bank, but for now, her friendship choices and adolescence cause her to feel and think differently. She might, in the future, dive into understanding and appreciating the Indian way of life, food and music given her current circumstances when she feels it is the right time to, and the same goes for her mother's Jamaican side of the family.

Dialogue and health cultural education

One way for her parents to deal with the matter is to introduce her to her relatives in either of her hometowns so she can see life there for herself and then make decisions that she feels best suits her. The complex dialogue interactions of humans with their surrounding world can be truly a challenge to untangle, but one way to make sense of our kids and their behavior is to help them break their experiences down into smaller meaningful units. Sometimes the world is not such a cruel place as their experiences make them think. Sarah's parents can use the narrative approach to describe their sets of experiences to their daughter for her to gain different perspectives on how inter-ethnic relations can take multiple faces. Such relations only benefit both sides and help people navigate the world together.

Within the classroom, teachers can help come up with coping strategies that help their students address issues surrounding how they dress, speak or act in class so they can help them comprehend classroom expectations and interactions better, to make them feel safer. Treating students from minority ethnic groups the same way they treat the rest of the kids will give Sarah the signal to start opening up about her true self. And who knows? You never know, someday she might be standing before the same kids she feared exposing herself to, but this time it would be her own self she would bring to Show and Tell. It will help her, as well as the other kids faced with the same cultural crisis, to become the active, engaged participants they deserve to be without having to leave their cultural identity.

Conclusion

This case study leaves us wondering more about Sarah. Did she conquer her fears? Is she still struggling but finding some peace in therapy? Did she leave her home to find her version of a safe haven, or has she started spending more time making the famous Jamaican jerk chicken with her mother? Does she celebrate Holi like never before, or is Christmas the only festival she takes pride in celebrating?

Key reflections

- o A cultural crisis can be used to refer to when someone no longer wishes to associate themselves with a particular culture.

- o Cultural add can be considered the act of embracing cultural traditions and heritage, actively incorporating them within lifestyle and identity.

- o Cultural fit leans towards reducing perceived difference with the aim to fit in more with the dominant, mainstream, or host culture and identity.

- o Teachers can encourage acceptance and help come up with coping strategies that help their students address issues surrounding how they dress, speak or act in class so they can help them comprehend classroom expectations and interactions better, to make them feel safer.

Pillar 2:
DIVERSITY

"It is our responsibility as adults to teach our children earlier on in life that there is beauty and strength in differences"
Dr. Gwanmesia.

Diversity is this book's second pillar, and this section builds upon our knowledge of culture and identity. Topics covered include the importance of diversity, types of diversity, and how diversity relates to the topics we've covered so far.

Chapter 4: Why Diversity Matters

What is diversity?

A broad definition of diversity would describe the existence of many different characteristics or elements among a group. Diversity is not limited to humanity; there can be diversity among other species or among inanimate objects. Diversity has more specific connotations related to gender, race, ethnicity, religion, ability, age, sexual orientation, socioeconomic status, educational level, and nationality.

When I think of dimensions what comes to mind is differences in communication styles, accents, languages, eye contact, tone of voice, what different communication mannerisms mean in different cultures for example, in my culture when talking to an elderly person, you are not supposed to maintain eye contact because that is considered disrespectful whereas in the United States you should maintain eye contact regardless of age. Let's point out these differences to our children as things that make us stronger, not weaker or less human.

When brought up in conversation, the word diversity is often accompanied by words such as equality, equity, or inclusion. This will be explored later in the book.

Dimensions of diversity and identity

The characteristics mentioned above represent difference, the variety of characteristics that make up our identities and life experiences. We can consider our own identity within these categories, and it is helpful to explore them beyond surface-level for a better understanding of ourselves or others. In the previous chapter, we discussed identity and how individuals can relate to multiple cultures at the same time, and that over time, this may change. We can consider diversity in a similar way. Many characteristics related to diversity (age, religion, sexuality, etc.) are not something we can choose or change.

An important dimension of diversity and identity is visibility and invisibility. Some differences may be outwardly identifiable, such as skin color, age, use of mobility aids, or religious symbols or clothing. Visible differences are noticeable to children at a young age. Perhaps you've been at the grocery store and your toddler asks, "Mom, why does she have brown skin?" or points to someone's wheelchair or hijab asking, "What is that?"

Moments such as these provide opportunities to discuss difference and diversity. But some may not be visible or identifiable from someone's appearance, and it is important to discuss those, too. For example, someone may have an invisible illness or disability, and their appearance and clothing may not reflect their social class, religion, or sexuality. Because of this, the people around us may be more diverse than we assume.

Why is it important to understand diversity?

Remembering that diversity and difference are varied and wide-ranging in scope and manifestation can help us avoid stereotyping others and making assumptions about their identity and experiences.

When young people understand what makes up "diversity", they can cultivate a stronger sense of identity, who they are, what makes them different from and similar to others. In turn, they can approach others with more respect, understanding, and open-mindedness. It is difficult, perhaps impossible, to conduct ourselves entirely independent of the stereotypes we learn and absorb. It also takes practice and conscious resistance to the associations and stereotypes that come to mind. But it is a mindset and approach that can benefit us all, and it is well worth fostering.

Diversity also exposes us to new perspectives, opinions, and ways of life. This broadens our own perspectives and worldviews and allows us to better understand others, empathize with others, and welcome and include others.

Practical ways of achieving diversity

You would find it funny how ironic it is that something that benefits society to this degree can be hard to achieve. Since the classroom is the second shared space after the family, where our children begin to cultivate their sense of self based on the transfer of ideas, learning, and dialogue across cultures, as teachers, we must consciously implement a curriculum that favors such differences. Since playtime can help incredibly with promoting interaction between the kids, including shapes and images of people from different potentials, ethnicities, and clothing in flash cards used for preschool children, or handouts and posters for the older ones can create an idea of acceptance and awareness. Guest speakers with real-life stories can help bring a different ideology to give a new pair of eyes and a fresh perspective to see the world. Sometimes moving away from the educational curriculum can help stimulate them and perk up their curiosity levels, irrespective of their ages.

Several Canadian schools have an Elder In-Residence program that collaborates with the school to help execute such an ideology (Iqbal, n.d.). During Open house Days or school visits, there are greetings, "hello" or "welcome," in different languages. But the linguistic diversity stops there, which feels like a missed opportunity for continued cultural connection in classrooms with linguistic diversity. Hanging signs, using labels, or presenting calendars in multiple languages is a common practice in some places, such as New Orleans, and the translations provide information as well as a reminder of cultural diversity. Games are also educational and playful ways to incorporate and teach about cultural or linguistic diversity. Resources and ideas are readily available online and can be as simple as adapting charades or bingo with everyday vocabulary in another language. When learning has an aspect of joy and fun, it is often to remember.

Children, their behavior, and the benefits of diverse experiences

I am sure many of us are fully, if not partially, acquainted with the concept of global pen pal friendships, where you can use numerous online platforms to connect the children to the country that intrigues them the most. It plays out the best for connecting classrooms that center around conventional American or English schooling and have little to no chance for inter-ethnic interactions within the system. When we can use dating apps or apps for general communication, such as Omegle, why not start thinking of innovative ideas along the same lines for possible healthy exposures for our kids?

How many of us craved field trips as kids or undergraduate students? I mean, who minds a day out with friends anyway, right? When having fun combined with an added touch of culture and enhancing your knowledge over it not just based on facts and figures but upon witnessing historical and cultural artifacts, it helps kids develop a more culturally diverse lens. Let us involve parents also in this journey and allow them to suggest better places they could go and trips they could take to unearth all the possibilities.

When we read books on parenting and socialization for our children, not a day goes by that we do not stumble over a section highlighting the importance of open communication. However, we rarely question the children about the list of prejudices they may have come across and create the resources to voice it out and share them with the community. A society similar to a support group can help bring everyone together, not just those enlisted to the council so that diverse opinions get brought to the forefront and talked about.

Remember that benefiting from diversity starts only when we learn to recognize it because deliberately staying oblivious to the existence of anything is similar to staying quiet over the wrong being done around us. And that is a world we should ever aspire to exist in.

Now staying oblivious does not necessarily have to come out in forms that we can directly observe. Sometimes, we unknowingly limit the complexities of our intellect by creating barricades to the meaning behind certain traditions we follow. Come to think of it, how many times have we played games like passing the parcel or Ring a Roses? But how many times have we pondered over the actual context and meaning behind some of the most universally used nursery rhymes? If we were to dive into their historical backgrounds, we would surprise ourselves at how we constantly and not knowingly accept diversity, be it in wordings or origins.

An interesting observation is that of the phrase "pass the parcel," which refers to a party game originating in Britain, which essentially only involved a gift wrapped in multiple types of paper that got passed around in successive rounds. The music playing in the background was the judge of this, in a way that it would randomly get interrupted, and the person with the gift at the time would lose the game in progression. It was the time mapped across several years, and its exposure to the different cultures tampered with the game a bit, either according to the available resources or to make it more simplified for the children to grasp. But what fascinates me most is how the concept got so universally accepted and used that its fundamentals lasted a lifetime.

Could you have ever imagined that a seemingly cherry rhyme, ring a Roses, could ever originate from an occasion as grim as the outbreak of the Great Plague in London in 1665? That is, in fact, true. When you read between the lines, you will realize the 'ring of roses' symbolized the red rash, which was one of the first signs for someone with the Bubonic and Pneumonic plague, and the "pocket full of posies" was something used for eliminating the odor that spread the disease. The cherry on top is the last part of the poem, which ends with everybody falling and talking about the sneezing and coughing before victims of the plague meet their final abode. Interesting or creepy? Maybe a bit of both but knowing something always makes way for knowledge and opens your eyes to the unknown realms of the world.

Millennials, Gen Z, and diversity

Recent generations have grown up with a much broader perspective of the world, in large part due to their connection to the internet. They are exposed to many cultures through both in-person and digital experiences, plus travel is much more accessible and affordable than it was for previous generations. As a result, many young people have broader, accepting views related to diversity, equality, inclusion, and matters of social justice (Parker, Graf, & Igielnik, 2019). While generalizations cannot apply across the board, their engagement with such subjects can be seen in political trends and protests, as well as their embrace of diverse practices in schools and workplaces.

We all have much to teach one another, and we can also learn a great amount from one another. As we raise the newest generation, we can look at the attitudes of Millennials and Gen Z and continue striving to build a world that is welcoming and accepting for all. Hopefully, our children can continue progress and ultimately achieve more peace and equality across the globe.

Sociological perspectives of diversity

Only when we provide the kids with a safe environment that favors equity and inclusivity within the classroom and disregards bullying, harassment, or discrimination can we begin to move above and beyond concepts of diversity itself. When children not only accept one another but wish to go as far as adopting some of the core values across cultures or learning life lessons from their inter-ethnic interactions, do we pave paths for authentic sociological research and methodology? Such research is integral if we wish to not stick to conventional versions of human thinking and behavior and go beyond what works in favor of society, which is to maintain the status quo because where humans exist, there will always be conflict. We must find ways to swim around the conflict to pull ourselves through it before drowning in the whims of others around us.

However, we would be doing the topic injustice if we were to stop here because let us face it. When was studying human interaction ever supposed to be easy? We would perhaps be fooling ourselves if we were to neglect the gray areas that surround the theories behind diversity and the consequences it has on social well-being.

There are three overarching theoretical orientations in the field of sociology: structural functionalism, symbolic interactionism, and conflict perspective (Cuff, Dennis, Francis, & Sharrock, 2016). If you were to see the world through the lens of a functionalist, it would give you a relatively black and white picture as opposed to a symbolic interactionist perspective. So, if you get offended quickly by seemingly conventional connotations, a functionalist sociologist might not be the way forward.

So, what exactly do they say that becomes such a matter of controversy? Perhaps the debate starts when they claim all social institutions are interdependent and that this feature can either make or break the stability of society. For instance, the workforce depends on the family to condition the children for a capitalist and exploitative society because that is the only way for individuals to survive in a competitive world. This conditioning eventually benefits the economy and helps people pay off their taxes and keep the cycling going endlessly, creating a generation of law-abiding, taxpaying citizens who unconditionally and conditionally benefit the state. While some connections drawn here make sense if one wishes to get a logical overview of the world, it promotes a stagnant, almost idealized perspective over how individuals think and behave.

In short, who is to decide what the correct form of living is? Who said that abiding by this repeated cycle is the only way you can sustain life in the society we live in today? When did maintaining the status quo become so integral that we started disregarding changes in behavioral patterns? How do we plan on benefiting from each other from our diverse skill sets or traditions if we were to shun the concept of individual differences altogether?

Such questions always bug me when I read about authors trying to present a perfect-looking world when we really should understand and grasp the beauty of diversity humans add to life. Unlike the functionalist framework, humans often do not find it easy to cope and work together in the workplace, school, or family. But we, as humans, must realize that we have the power to channel this conflict of interest, power, and thought and behavior to our advantage. The power of conflict, ironically, is that it can bring peace and growth if used smartly.

There is no surprise that functionalism receives ample backlash from contrasting sociological views in today's world, such as from symbolic interactionism. As the name suggests, interactionists support the conflict theory, where they acknowledge the ever-changing, fickle nature of society which has its benefits, as mentioned previously, but also recognize the presence of negativity (Cuff, Dennis, Francis, & Sharrock, 2016). For instance, marriage is an institution that might not always be as smooth sailing as described by the functionalist theory and can often result in divorce or separation. And where there exists a conflict, there exists social change.

The social interactionist perspective encourages individuals to play an active role in changing their external environment especially when it benefits them. For instance, if a norm disregards the presence of a value followed in another culture in a humiliating way, an individual has every right to speak against it and wish for it to be changed, even if it challenges the status quo and does not promise social stability. According to sociologists following the same ideology, human interaction would be impossible without the use of meaningful communication and symbols, such as language. Therefore, they consider society a product of shared symbols brought about through the meanings individuals give to events constantly happening around them, which shapes their identity and helps with the acceptance of diversity within the community.

Similarly, it is common in French culture to shake hands but to kiss those close to you on both the cheeks with a greeting described as *la bise*, again showing appreciation but in a very different way, which you never get to see in other cultures. The two times can also sometimes stretch out to three when Muslims exchange three hugs on

Eid, which can be categorized as both religious and cultural.

One of the students suggested that asking a question not of the highest caliber could be embarrassing for themselves and offensive to the teacher (Carter, 2006). The reason was that it would make them look like the problem, meaning there was some setback in their tutoring methodology. Therefore, all instructions were considered correct and standard by the kids unconditionally, not open to any form of interpretation.

Another concern that made the Asian students think twice before uttering a word in the class was if whatever they brought to the forefront were of any value to the others in the class (Carter, 2006). Therefore, they mostly kept their questions for the end but finding a question was also rare since it hardly ever fit into their list of standards during their desperate attempts to support existing norms for smoothly operating the curriculum. On the pro side, since learning was an individual experience for these kids, they worked independently and often secured the best grades.

Such disparities made it harder for the students to understand each other, such as the American children thought a lack of class participation of the Asians directly translated to a shorter attention span. However, it is up to the teachers to give the students a chance to voice their own experiences and overcome any cultural or language barriers that may prevent them from speaking openly and being unapproachable to the children. On the positive side, in the case study, the Asian students were impressed with how lively and laid back some teachers were and how thoroughly prepared they were with their daily lessons. They appreciated such a change because it seemed refreshing to them in relation to their teachers back home, who only came to school to finish their jobs and get their paychecks. Little did they care about establishing a rapport with the children, and the most unfortunate outcome was that children came to perceive and accept those versions as realities that they had to cope with (Carter, 2006).

The United States is a diverse country with a wide range of cultures, nationalities, and languages represented throughout. While it is typically referred to as a "melting pot," I prefer the metaphor of a salad bowl. Instead of all ultimately blending together and losing aspects of our identity as we integrate past the point of recognizable individuality, I see value in keeping aspects of our individuality. Teaching our children about diversity opens them up to new perspectives and experiences, and it can lead to a deeper love for our fellow humans––something that can have a deep and widespread transformative effect.

Key reflections:

- o Remembering that diversity and difference are varied and wide-ranging in scope and manifestation can help us avoid stereotyping others and making assumptions about their identity and experiences.

- o Diversity also exposes us to new perspectives, opinions, ways of life, and more. This broadens our own perspectives and worldviews and allows us to better understand others, empathize with others, and welcome and include others.

Chapter 5: Modern-day Culture, Diversity, and Identity

When we begin to understand diversity beyond conventional definitions, we begin to observe how the rebranding of different companies to become more sensitive to the needs of inter-ethnic groups has helped individuals gain better values. Sodexo is one such company that hired its first chief diversity officer, Anand Rohini, who diversified the company's fundamentals; gender, ethnicity, disabilities, and age. This system shift, to introduce new human resources policies, such as flexibility measures, training, selection processes, and career services for people of all origins, helped change its overall mindset. The diversity seen in the gender department also encouraged more women and minority groups to contribute to the company by taking on leadership positions. It made Sodexo stand out as a diversity champion by 2005 (Thomas & Creary, 2012).

We talked about diversity according to different sociological perspectives, but what if I were to tell you the conflict of opinion has only just started? Diversity is just one of the causes to lead to even broader concerns that receive greater debate and controversy.

Let us put it this way. How many of us find it hard to shift to a new place, adjust to the gears of a new car, or even get used to seeing ourselves after getting a balayage? Is not a hard pill to swallow? Multiply that to a few degrees to what individuals living within any society face when it goes through social change, irrespective of the degree of change in question.

An analytical approach to understanding social change

So, what name do we give to social change, and how do we make sense of it? When we consider diversity as an acceptance of behaviors, mannerisms, and thought processes that can help bring the community together, are we suggesting that diversity helps connect the world? In that case, we can conclude that cultural diversity leads to a process of globalization that has made the world more interdependent. Consider the example of a spider web stretching across a greater scale over time. The increase in the number and threads of the web are the cultural values bleeding across a multitude of societies. A range of products could constitute the threads, be it people, money, material goods, thoughts, or even disease and suffering that now travel faster than ever. The COVID-19 pandemic is a shining example of this where a disease originating in one region of the world spread worldwide, with its rapidity leaving people confused and helpless at the hands of globalization. On the one hand, where life is not possible anymore without technology and travel, it also becomes a source of trouble and loss of control in the world we know today. Perhaps it is another idea that falls under the list of the many ironic ways the world works.

Globalization and its effects

Narrowing globalization to just the cultural variety, we find that it is only a fancy terminology to describe the transfer of ideas, meanings, and values in a way that favors deeper social relations. The catalyst in this process mainly is the internet, popular culture media, and the tourism industry.

The world has become more cosmopolitan since people get freely woven into the strange mix of cultural threads, so much so that it is hard to pull one apart from the other. The greater frequency of air travel has led to foreign embassies fostering positive relations between countries and growing the tourist industry to welcome people to their host country from all over the world. The news has always stayed one of the most effective ways of broadcasting ideas to the world, but only recently has it grown wings since the growth of media and online platforms with uploaded channels that make information all the more accessible. Subtitles and dubbing have allowed even better communication and helped combine languages and news channels to fulfill the agenda of keeping it as local as possible in terms of branches and language.

As we discussed before, education has led to a shift in cultural expression, which affects thinking patterns and new ideologies to take action. For instance, take the classic example of Western individualism versus collectivism found in much of the rest of the world. A study showed how an introduction to the English language in Chinese curricula led to the presence of deductive reasoning exhibited by the local students (Liu, 2012). Reading and writing the new language gave them further insights into American and English culture, which developed a sense of individualism and freedom of thinking by studying American lifestyles and opening their eyes to the whims of the world around them.

Most of the entertainment we consume, be it Netflix or movie channels such as HBO, contains English content. While most of these have subtitles in several languages for those not well-versed with the language, they still face a shift in cultural values and beliefs, some even taking a U-turn from local cultural values, often even opposing the culture of origin.

For instance, the multitude of English shows and films in the Philippines causes several people, especially the Gen Z crowd, to take on the new language as their own and leave their native behind. When they see actors on the red carpet, living their dream lives, and flashing their privilege about, all they wish to do is to sound and dress like them. Perhaps it is this need or desire to come at par with their role models which causes dominance of a host culture as a result of globalization. Think of this: How many of us have heard Dua Lipa speak in one of her recent interviews where we wished our British English could sail as smoothly as the words flowing out of her?

The process of globalization, when seen from a broader perspective, can seem appealing in the freedom it provides at an individual level, but it may not always play out the way we would expect it to. The clash between cultures can cause a 'global culture' to emerge, with one culture gaining precedence over others, weakening the local ones. While, on the one hand, globalization makes people think outside the box and challenge prevalent stereotypes and prejudicial belief systems, it can also create a clash between personalities.

Many sociologists agree the postmodern world has led to the growth of a "consumer culture", where individuals are typically like customers shopping in a market, free to pick and choose the product (identity) they wish to clothe themselves with (Study Smarter, n.d.). Therefore, individuals find themselves immersed in belief systems they never thought they would feel convinced to explore or even try on different pieces of clothing they never thought they would enjoy wearing.

Consumer goods like coffee did not exist as universally as they do now. It first originated from Ethiopia, in the Arabian community. It was not until the 11th century that commercial trades turned it into a globally used commodity. Similarly, avocados first grew in the city of Mexico because the tropical temperatures of the Dominican Republic favored its cultivation, but today it is supplied to even the local communities. And having avocados on toast is one of the most popular breakfasts worldwide. Festivals such as Black Friday in the US, the Brazilian Carnival, Indian Holi Festival, Christmas, and the Eid festival for Muslims have gained recognition in several parts of the world because of the evolving tourist culture. Such festivals might hold different meanings on different continents, but their mission of bringing communities together remains grounded.

In understanding the drawbacks of globalization in contemporary society, we focus on how the merging of different cultures creates a simultaneous threat to the other respective traditions in a way that has homogenized the world's cultures. As a result, particular cultural properties are faced with a decline, starting from languages to traditions or to even specific industries. That is why protecting cultural values must consciously get implemented in a globalized world to preserve this treasure of cultural values.

Perhaps when we grow older, we realize why our parents' implemented rules in the house to only converse in the native language even when, to our adolescent minds, it seemed 'uncool' to not converse in English. People often realize how valuable it is to take your culture along later on in their lives, when we start agreeing with sociologists such as Ulrich Beck. He claims that the ever-changing global world of today might appear smaller to us because of how connected the lives of individuals are to each other (Beck, 2006). However, our perceptions evolve at a much slower pace than we think as we strive to still hold onto our old national demarcations, which again brings us to the concept of the "*us vs. them*" notion.

So where does one stand in a place where the arguments surrounding globalization seem to contradict one another and make it even more difficult to know who you truly wish to become? How do we convince ourselves to know more about the world in trying to figure ourselves out so we can better guide our kids when every new thought leaves us more perplexed than ever? What products do we pick and choose which create the best fit for ourselves and our children?

Perhaps the answers to questions like these are much easier to figure out than we think, but we instead try to wade through them wearing a blindfold, forgetting that the solutions lie in the problems themselves. If we feel threatened by a dominant culture for our children, we can find ways to limit their access to certain websites over the internet. It reduces the likeliness of exposure to mature content or content that might deter them from their belief structures. If technology is the monster under your bed, use it to your advantage and take charge. However, such ways only play out till a certain age, after which individuals must get the space to grow the wings to fly to their nests and frame their own lives around them.

But as humans are influenced in the blink of an eye, it is almost impossible to save ourselves from the effects of the outside world, and sooner or later, we will have to peek through our shells and experience it the way it is. Since the conflict of topic causes a good amount of concern and irony, it has slowly become a hot topic and even gets termed "the most widely discussed hallmark of global culture" (Jennings, 2011). Since multinational media and global culture hold immense power over people, they can erode whole cultures through their impact. And it may not come as a surprise to you that it mostly gets used in the context of Western culture threatening the existence of others.

If we speak of the growing economy in the West and its notorious cultural effects, nine out of ten chances are that your mind is bound to wander towards capitalist culture, which slowly conditions individuals to become slaves to the exploitative world. Such a process has led to a McDonaldization or Westernization of ideas (George Ritzer, 1993). Many indigenous cultures found it hard to come to terms with such major shifts in ideology, while others favored it, since they support the concept of conventional thinking being allowed no space to foster in modern society. This thought holds valid for the most part because humans are free to make their choices while still staying aware and ready to face the consequences of those decisions.

Cultural homogenization and heterogenization

Like bricks making a whole wall, the idea of cultural breakdown and influence brings us to the process of homogenization, which refers to a reduction in cultural diversity (of local cultures) through the popularization and diffusion of a range of cultural symbols, customs, ideas and values. Some say that this growth can never stay one way, meaning that the bleeding out of different ways of life into each other can never render one as dominant and the other suppressed. Hence, some sociologists have concluded cultural homogenization is not a process that invalidates a particular set of cultural values, but it makes people aware of diverse forms of living. Many say that it is nothing but a generalization to assume cultural homogenization always starts in the western world. A popularization of non-American culture can also, in turn, affect Western thought processing and ideology like the influence of Latin American shows, Japanese anime, Indian Bollywood, or Korean dramas, pop culture or cuisine, such as the famous Korean chicken now available at every other restaurant.

But since globalization is an umbrella term for all issues such as these, it is not possible for there to be a transfer and adoption of elements from a global to a local culture. The conflict boils down to the opposing concepts of cultural homogenization and cultural heterogenization.

Building cultural intelligence in understanding diversity

When we talk about emotional intelligence and the change in worldwide dynamics, we essentially refer to tackling problems of inclusivity that bleed into the workplace from the classroom environment. The need for understanding cross-cultural knowledge over the market aids in better marketing of products and for companies to work smarter. When companies do not hire native speakers to devise culturally sensitive translations for their websites and brochures, they sow the seed for failure.

A typical example of this is the KFC chicken marketed in China with the tagline indicating it to be so tasty, you will "eat your fingers off!" Now as hilarious as this might sound, it is a poor, almost offensive translation of the original brand tagline, "Finger-lickin' good" (Dass & Vinnakota, 2019). The same goes for slogans or posters in local areas that could seem confusing to outsiders. Therefore, in the same way that hiring a diverse set of teachers can increase the knowledge of inter-ethnic students within a classroom, serious market blunders also can be easily mitigated by hiring a diverse workforce. If you want cultures to gel well together, you must work towards healthier, more effective ways to maintain it.

One of the many reasons why a global shift makes it almost impossible for people to benefit from a diverse pool of talent without being inclusive is because it can otherwise get hard to keep globally minded, ambitious candidates on board. Such diversity must move beyond bookish definitions of gender, religion, and ethnicity to ensure a safe, diverse workplace. Such workplaces produce respected and valued workers with a long-lived loyalty to the company.

As is obvious, a safe passage would involve keeping your students or workers as homogenous as possible to keep a peaceful contribution to the status quo going. But in a globalized, highly competitive environment, boxing an ocean full of ideas and sealing the doors to creative thought and action will seriously hamper societal growth, as well as reduce the lifetime of any company. Healthy competition is vital to keep the efficiency of any institution running at its optimum level. It is only possible when the challenges of working with a diverse group of individuals become the drive helping them perform better. Fighting off and bonding over negative stereotyping can help similarities and differences translate into you becoming a global citizen to combat an unrealistic ethnocentric worldview.

Overcoming restrictions in a culturally fluid space

As much as the globalized world has helped the tourist industry evolve by accelerating local and international travel, it also implements restrictions, such as employment laws and visa requirements, especially for international workers. Such requirements in workplaces must be fulfilled if we wish to retain a culturally fluid environment. Assigning a separate prayer room for students or workers who feel the need to take time out for it during school/work hours irrespective of their beliefs could be one step towards bringing the communities together. Or taking into consideration that people need a couple of days off from work or school for important ritual holidays, like Eid, Diwali, Holi, Christmas, or Easter, could create a more aware and inclusive space. We sometimes focus too much on issues such as gender inclusivity, which still has a long way to go and is equally important but must not overshadow cultural variation. If we can impose maternity leave for better ease to working women, we can easily consider giving a couple of days off to the respective employees too, and not invalidate their basic demands and rights.

In conclusion, when inherited and achieved social identities come face to face in terms of differing status or value, people use a list of coping mechanisms to resolve this conflicted state. At times, they get rid of a particular identity altogether and integrate or fuse more than one identity together (Berry & Sabatier, 2011). Politicized or opinion-based discussions within a classroom system can form new opinions and fluid identities that can potentially increase distress.

People's sense of self revolves around four major groupings in terms of roles (a student), relational (a friend), or socially created ones (nationality). Some of the most observed forms of identity management that become a byproduct of such a crisis involve reconciliation, retreat, realignment, and reflection. The effects of such behaviors can intensify or diminish based on compatibility levels between several cultural affiliations, which is why we must always practice kindness and empathy. You really do not know what someone might be going through, they could be falling off a cliff and pretend not a word affects them.

Key reflections:

- o Globalization can seem appealing in the freedom it provides at an individual level, but it may not always play out the way we would expect it to. The clash between cultures can cause a "global culture" to emerge, with one culture gaining precedence over others, weakening the local ones.

- o Globalization makes people think outside the box and challenge prevalent stereotypes and prejudicial belief systems. But it can also create a clash between personalities.

- o In understanding the drawbacks of globalization in contemporary society, we focus on how the merging of different cultures creates a simultaneous threat to the other respective traditions in a way that has homogenized the world's cultures.

Pillar 3:
EQUITY

"We are all creative, but by the time we are three or four years old, someone has knocked the creativity out of us. Some people shut up the kids who start to tell stories. Kids dance in their cribs, but someone will insist they sit still. By the time the creative people are ten or twelve, they want to be like everyone else."

Maya Angelou

Chapter 6: Equity and Identity

Concerning the previous chapter, would you then conclude the end purpose behind creating a safer space for individuals and making opportunities available to all is to water the purpose of attaining equality, or perhaps cultural equity? But what puts these two categories apart, or is it more of a to-may-to, to-mah-to situation? Can one exist without the other, or does the beauty lie in this fact itself that two things that sound so similar exist better independently?

Equality vs. equity

Most books mention the word equality, and it is easy to find factual definitions, but when we drift away from what is factual and more one directional in meaning, matters tend to get slightly complicated. When individual differences actively intervene in our definitions of the world, we begin to question the very meanings we give to it and slowly etch closer towards a possible early life crisis. At times, we go on an endless train of thought over what cultural values mean, but seldom do we sit down to think of the psychological safety inclusivity can nurture and the sense of belonging it has the power to create.

That is when cultural equity kicks in since it encapsulates, celebrates, and represents all values, policies, and practices including all individuals, (not just limited to the underrepresented minority groups), based on factors like race/ethnicity, age, disability, sexual orientation, gender, gender identity, socioeconomic status, geography, religion or citizenship status. In short, having a level playing field for creativity and opportunities for everyone is the goal behind such a theory. Such an agenda can only nr made possible by a strategic distribution of programmatic, financial, and informational resources.

Speaking of equality, then how does it take a different route from what we talked about above? The term equality deals with justice and sameness between individuals or groups within society and favors equal treatment and resources between them. On the other hand, to achieve equity, one does not treat all groups equally, but based on their need and situation, and then distributes the resources based on such information amongst the many groups to reach the most ideal outcome for all of them.

Consider this situation to make better sense of the relationship. A plant growing in ideal conditions with ample water and sunlight produces enough fruit and shows no signs of deficiency. Now compare that to one growing in a drier climate with inadequate rainfall to give it the backbone it needs. Now if a person were to manually water just one plant since he only has enough for one, it would be the smartest thing to do since it leads to optimum growth for both plants, giving them an equal opportunity to grow well and strive, producing ample fruits. What the person did here was not divide his resources equally but judge the need and input required based on their scenarios and privilege. Now more people can benefit from the fruit and shade in the vicinity, and everyone reaps the results.

One thing to remember here while drawing similarities between two apple trees and society besides their difference in scope is that while a tree exists in a naturally occurring system, a social system may not. That does not mean society was designed to be naturally inequitable. Instead, it is essentially crafted to favor specific demographics but what makes outcomes play out differently is the existence of discriminatory practices and belief systems that have created rifts between social groups.

Surprised at this remarkable difference between the two? So was I when I first came across them, since at first glance, one can get fooled into believing they are all the same. Perhaps we are not to blame for such a misconception since the twin terms get used together in matters regarding the law, government, and economics to describe actions, laws, or rules devised to eradicate unjust and unfair treatment. However, while their definitions might seem alike, the means to achieve them take a very different course. The word equality is translated as "the state or quality of being equal concerning degree, value, rank, or ability" (Dictionary.com, 2020). When used in court, such as in America, it pertains to the notion that all people have access to their rights regardless of their talents or differences. Therefore, it expresses qualities of being fair or impartial, or impartial.

The problem starts when people demand to be allowed to define what meanings 'just' and 'fair' hold for them. Since these are subjective concepts, they require immense consideration and pondering over, which puts even law firms at unease when a concept like this gets brought to the forefront. One of the many reasons the controversy has increased is because of people's frustration for their kids at school or for themselves at the workplace over the years where they supposedly have access to equal rights but still do not receive proper treatment. It goes especially for the historically oppressed groups such as LGBTQ+ people, black people, and the indigenous who feel half their lives get spent asking for what legally should be theirs.

As sad as this sounds, it is best to accept that it will be challenging for equity to follow suit of equality and vice versa. When we socialize our kids into understanding the world, concepts like these can help them treat others around them better and more appropriately. Maybe we should not expect our children to exhibit any level of altruism or to consider people's motives and actions as selfless, for there hardly exists a thing such as this. But we could instill in them the emotional intelligence to understand the ways of the world and work accordingly. As teachers, when we talk about their biased treatment or unrealistic assumptions towards minority groups, or a lack of resources for the disabled in the school or curriculum, are we not directly pointing towards a lack of equity? Ironically, the solution to most problems is the lack of the very thing itself. When we speak of making classrooms more culturally inclusive, or the need for teachers to go the extra mile for kids trying to fit into a host culture, we essentially suggest countering a lack of equity with equity.

The best part is that you do not have to take on the role of a mother or tutor to be able to embrace the concept of offering fair treatment to all groups based on the financial hierarchy. Architectural engineers worldwide have devised ways to make institutions more inclusive to the disabled by giving preferential treatment to meet their needs. It is a given that places like hospitals feature the convenience of a ramp and wheelchairs because it essentially caters to the old, diseased, or injured. But when was the last time you got to see a wheelchair at your university? So what does a person do when they literally break a leg or sprain an ankle so badly they cannot put up with their gait? Additionally, how are those with intellectual disabilities or mental health issues accommodated and supported?

We would feel surprised at how common it is for places to walk around wearing the card of equity tied around their necks, but it hardly ever gets practically implemented to generate real solutions. Equity goes well beyond adopting characteristic values and only fully comes to life with years of commitment, investment of resources, and a smart distribution of them.

Suppose a school in Northern Virginia has too restricted a space to accommodate the cumulative numbers of students enrolled and is on the verge of collapse. Another elementary school in the same district has a newer and better-constructed foundation, needs little to no maintenance, and contains enough area to hold the staff and children, providing them with a space to operate in. When the school county district receives annual demographics, they decide to allocate a greater percentage of the funds towards building a new school in place of the dilapidated building to put the property in better, safer usage. The newer school receives a smaller fund in comparison because it already looks like it is on the right track. This approach did not just provide a safe, healthy environment to all the students but also gave a message to their parents that the kids would be promised quality education and basic rights irrespective of how capable they were to pay for those privileges.

Equity is indeed a strange terminology because once you consciously begin to welcome it with open arms, it unintentionally gives you the tools to fight the most stubborn of your demons. If the teacher shares their most intimate, most challenging encounters with their kids who need their inspiration the most, what they essentially do is choose to embrace their unique backgrounds and historical encounters, so the kids do the same, and they pass on the same energy and attitudes ahead.

According to a teaching professor in Northeastern University's College of Professional Studies, classrooms are works in progress where to practice equity, we must let identities and locations play their part in helping us form healthier perspectives on each other (DiFranza, 2019). One way to get started in an approach like this is to try matching teaching styles to their origins and make the kids understand how mutual and diverse experiences can help shape their learning experiences better without even considering it a problem teachers need to manage.

Why equity must become the central feature of classrooms

In a world full of post-Millennials, it is not a surprise that teachers find it harder to cope with the ever-increasing fluidity and polarity of identities as different worlds constantly collide together. Such issues have always remained very real, but most of the recent breakthroughs in society have opened ways to new versions of thinking, making significant portions of the masses realize such issues need to be spoken about even if they do not directly affect or influence them.

Since the kids of today are the future of tomorrow, their perspectives, when shining through, help teachers implement better, more influential strategies. The youth of today does not wish to stay blindfolded in an idealized world full of a simulation of sorts, or pretend to understand the situation as a color-blind, class-blind, or gender-blind reality. They wish to accept it in its worst, most crude forms, which goes further than just the notion of bland diversity and inclusion, which makes them ready and open to arguing about ways in making issues of equity and power dynamics as the lighthouse guiding classroom interactions and identity formation.

Effective strategies for implementing equity

Such guidelines do not have a set magic recipe to follow and nor do they promise everlasting results but can guarantee some relief to an effective learning environment. The goal is to promote a tone of equality for everyone involved. The act of "calling in" any insensitive comments by the teacher after carefully detecting instances of bias, oppression, and other subconscious or conscious identity-based assumptions and ideas that get brought up within student interactions, can replace the old strategy of "calling them out" on something that they themselves cannot make sense of or know whether to agree on. This strategy is a tried and tested one, by a practicing professor, Attwood, who says it brought her effective results by not putting the kid on the spot or making him feel bad for putting his thoughts out in an offensive way (DiFranza, 2019). It merely involved bringing attention to the comment and interrupting discussion by questioning the children about the rights and wrongs of it and attending to the issue head-on. It allows an inclusive way of dissecting the problem and helps others around to understand the context of the comment, based on the commenter's experiences and background that could have triggered the bias.

The teacher must devise ways where she can make it known to the class exactly what is going on, in terms of recognizing, listing, and naming the situation and dialogue at hand while feeling comfortable establishing how singular instances or a pattern of misfortunes can cause people to react differently to situations. Recognizing some apparent differences in such sociological processes can help us break free from the shackles of subconscious ideas because like equity, to unlearn patterns, we must first learn them.

Communicating classroom standards

Creating a degree of discomfort by exposing the students to opinions contrary to popular beliefs while still operating in a safe space can help them evolve from their caterpillar stage since emotional stimulation always causes the mind to grow. Students must know they have the power and authority to speak their hearts out and that their words will have equal significance in terms of holding productivity in conversation. When the quieter voices do not feel silenced but receive an effective license to communicate, they might have more to bring to the table when resolving matters of equity than those who appear more vocal.

The proverb, "We have two ears and one mouth, so we should listen more than we say" seems most fitting to the occasion because the more we encourage our kids to listen to another's perspectives before jumping in to defend themselves or highlight their experiences, the more we can help them make use of an equitable environment. Setting the right tone to discuss such delicate ideas by the instructor can indicate to the kids that asking questions and viewing confusion and discomfort forms an integral part of learning and helps them overcome those same problems. It makes the teacher look more "approachable," especially to the marginalized majority. Remember, if you get the honor of working across cultures, you must remind yourself that something powerful is on your way because the diversity represented has the power to grant you the opportunity to learn in the midst of the social tension created.

Beyond the responsibility of educators

It's very easy to point fingers at those visibly running the system––the teachers, but it would not be fair to lay all responsibility on their shoulders. There are more prominent figures running the institution who exercise power and influence over the set curriculum policies and who hold authority in tweaking the system. The students and organization must intervene in aiding the process by striving for intellectual humility and inclusiveness by standing confidently in their own shoes of individual perspectives backed by tolerance for others and informed knowledge that comes from perceptual experiences and study. In short, the spark of curiosity should never be allowed to fade.

On the level of an organization, equal life chances would mean not letting those aspects of individuals get in the way of their opportunities for matters they cannot control. A fair way to enroll students on meritocratic standards could help render all socioeconomic differences, void. A system of fair competition that favors talent, hard work, and ability can help solve the problem to maintain equal competition. The reason for us to highlight such an issue is that whatever we discussed above cannot be brought to light when the very system running it cannot replace privilege with equity for all.

Cultural gatekeeping is a phenomenon we categorize as another con in today's globalized world, where the big fish in any system exercise absolute control in suggesting how resources and power dynamics spread across different groups. We see such concepts exercised in cultural values as well, where critics and educators decide what is worthy or acceptable for mentioning in the classroom. It is a particularly dangerous threat to the organization and can invite significant levels of opposition and social exclusion. Such intergenerational transmissions across formal and informal institutions result in social inequity and chronic poverty across generations. It is almost frightening to see how much of a worrying picture inequitable access to resources and services can create and the impact it has on life chances and how much people can sometimes have to rely on inherited circumstances.

Therefore, a targeted action towards disadvantaged groups, such as special quotas to provide employment or funds cashed in an elementary school for girls, can help empower individuals to a huge scale. A "downstream" action to regulate resources following equity to counter inequality and provide social security, can be particularly hard to achieve (in the presence of an oppressive ruling body or clashing ideology), but also immensely rewarding simultaneously.

The cultural iceberg model: a ray of hope?

Just like diving into the organization of any system can help give us a better grip over the situation, diving under the surface of society can help cater to most social problems, even those that are cultural and more stubborn to excavate. The external or conscious part of culture is the one we can visibly see and process, including visible behaviors and institutionalized belief systems. But unconscious culture takes up the face of belief systems and values which extend over thought processes and define behavior.

Figure 1-The Iceberg

Edward T. Hall's Cultural Iceberg Model promotes such an ideology, which is a tool that helps one shift their perspective beyond what the eye can see, or the submerged part of the iceberg that's not visible below its tip (Hall, 1976). The tip of the iceberg, Hall posits, is the 10% of culture that is easily visible. These external, or surface-level, factors include behaviors, traditions, and customs. For the most part, these are explicitly learned, conscious, easily changeable, and related to objective knowledge. The submerged part of the iceberg, on the other hand, is the other 90%. These parts of culture can be considered deeper, more internalized aspects, such as core values, beliefs, priorities, attitudes, assumptions, and perceptions. They're more difficult to pinpoint since they cannot be observed with our senses; they're unconscious, implicitly learned, difficult to change, and related to subjective knowledge. Hall's theory of the cultural iceberg is a helpful strategy for considering the multifaceted nature of cultural identity. The iceberg can also be a helpful visual aid in a classroom, and students can be encouraged to reflect upon their own cultural icebergs.

When we talked about teachers staying more alert and sensitive to cultural bias in the classroom, it was yet another way to help extract the root causes behind why such interactions occur. As we already know, unconscious biases come out as social stereotypes on certain groups of people that often have little to do with their own awareness.

According to Hall, cultural aspects above the water constitute only a minuscule portion of the values making up the bigger picture beyond the surface. An effective design for retaining the students by boosting their sense of self through equity can help us shift the curriculum to the ICEBERG model, which stands for Integrated, Collaborative, Engaging, Balanced, Economical, Reflective, and Gradual forms of teacher-student relations (van Ameijde & Weller, 2015). Ever heard the phrase, "Don't judge a book by its cover"? Let us take our own advice here and not judge a culture with the way it first appears to be because, while it is true everyone cannot be cut out for the same cultural values, we can at least respect those who choose to lead their lives a different way by interacting with them more.

An example of this is the onion analogy, where the core of the onion is the culture determining the many layers of tangible outer layers of abstract ideas. The submerged tip of the iceberg represents unattended values and assumptions that are fundamental blocks essential to being studied for understanding attitudes and conventions, which are accepted behaviors. Such as a preference to eat rice using your hands could be an acquired cultural attitude that evokes feelings of comfort for someone.

So, the next time we see someone clad from head to toe in an outer additional garment, let us not make irrational conclusions on social issues like oppression and gender segregation. What we can instead do, is utilize such religious or cultural symbols to understand symbolic behaviors that stem from them. When you sit with a group of people sharing the intricacies of the same culture, you realize the actual ideology stemming from historical legendary figures and several man-made artifacts, where the products are tools high in cultural significance. Perhaps a woman who chooses to cover herself up around other men considers practicing her will as a source of empowerment or just a way to present her identity irrespective of whichever religion she comes from. We often talk about inclusivity, such as showing less skin, as a matter of personal freedom, but you would be surprised to see how stringent some schools and people are in implementing such an ideology. Some schools put up official rules preventing the girls from wearing a pair of leggings under their skirts, even if their bare legs make them feel uncomfortable and triggers their insecurities.

Perhaps peeling away at the layers of hidden identities can help bridge cultural differences and become a solution in making the world a more pleasant place to live.

"Single stories" and the pyramid of hate: a case study

Yes, the term is quite relevant to forming opinions on cultural practices, and no, it would have been totally absurd if I were to talk about real estate here. The phrase "single stories" describes an exceptionally simplistic perception that produces a false and inadequate opinion over someone, be it individuals, groups, or companies. Chimamanda Ngozi Adichie, an author from Nigeria, narrates short stories to shed light on some of her enlightening experiences dealing with a few conscious and unconscious ways she either was influenced or influenced others due to inadequate information and exposure (Adichie, 2012).

We often make the mistake of only paying attention to one side of the world of existing perspectives and basing our lives on that single experience. The default assumptions that result from such opinions do not just create a truckload of misunderstandings but can have long-lasting damage to inter-cultural interaction and labeling.

She starts off by narrating her early childhood life where she was well-acquainted with reading and writing, believing she had understood the world enough to write about it. But what she did not know was how an honest picture of the world was miles away from her illustrated characters, who all had typical blue eyes, white faces, frolicking around in the snow, eating apples, with the weather being their most major concern. Since Adichie had only lived in the same four walls in Nigeria for all those seven years, you would wonder how she developed a worldview so different from her way of life, where people never experienced anything close to the snow, only ate mangoes, and hardly ever thought the weather to be a topic problematic enough to be discussed.

Perhaps when we speak of culture, we often forget how easily impressed and vulnerable children can be through literature, and how powerful story narration is in shaping their minds to the newness of the world they try to discover. Since the author had only ever come across books depicting foreigners with lives entirely different to her own, writing, to her, was only those books that, by their nature, had to reflect stories and characters she could hardly personally identify. However, when she realized there existed books celebrating her culture as it had always deserved to be, it shifted her perspective on literature, that brown girls like her with kinky hair could also be brought into the limelight much the same way. Such a shift helped her move away from her "single story" on storytelling and once when she felt pride in her origins, did she truly begin to appreciate American and British as doorways to open up new worlds for her while still helping her overcome those preconceived, damaging notions.

Her later experiences moving into further education are evidence of how many affiliations to a mix of cultures can go a long way. When she moved in with an American roommate at 19, she surprised her friend with her fluency in English and her friend was shocked out of her wits to know it was the national language of Nigeria. As bizarre as this sounds, she did not expect Adichie to have a good hand at it at all due to her "single story" assumption for Africans to be *poor* and *backward*, which came off as almost patronizing to the author at first. Such labeling is damaging in itself since it seeks to seal all and any possibility for feelings outside of pity and forms no connection to humans as equals. However, Adichie later realized no one was to blame, because if she had only experienced her homeland only through pictures, her version of it would only have beautiful landscapes and animals, people fighting senseless wars, poverty-stricken areas, and AIDS, with helpless people waiting for "white privilege" to come to their aid, with only gloom and doom ahead of them.

When narrating real-life stories of ourselves or those who inspire us to our children, we must stay alert for potential "single stories" by addressing our power. Power in this context pertains to a word from the Nigerian language, "Igbo," which translates "to be greater than another," and in order to practice this, we should stay wary of how and when we tell our stories. Perhaps the beauty lies in the power of this concept when inspiring others. Just like African culture, all cultures go through a multitude of issues, but only sticking to the negative stories can flatten your experiences greatly and the stereotypes created are not just untrue, but also incomplete, since the one version of story they create becomes instrumental to a lack of equality. For instance, if Adichie's roommate had known about a Nigerian publisher who left his job to focus on his dreams of becoming a publisher, or the Nigerian female lawyer who took the ridiculous idea of taking her husband's consent before renewing her passport to the courts, she would not have formed such a biased opinion on her Nigerian heritage.

When people focus too much on establishing differences and prejudices amongst each other, the Pyramid of Hate comes alive, which eventually leads to larger problems like genocide, illustrated by the prevalence of societal bias, hate, and oppression (Anti-Defamation League, 2018). Just like a pyramid, the upper levels are influenced by the ones below and bias at every stage creates a whole system of oppression. When it is "normalized" for people to experience conventional biases across cultures, they get conditioned into believing it as 'normal' and "natural," which even convinces them to hold back on their true versions of identity and suppress who they truly are. Therefore, we must engage our children and give them the weapons they need to hold their own and challenge such biased attitudes so they can fight off discrimination. Let us not allow issues like 'single story' worldviews to strip our children of dignity, which can come to a point where they find it almost impossible to take humanity and equality together.

Key reflections:

- o Equity seeks to create a level playing field by a strategic distribution of programmatic, financial, and informational resources.

- o Classrooms are works in progress where to practice equity, we must let identities and locations play their part in helping us form healthier perspectives on each other.

- o The cultural iceberg model gives us a tool to consider cultural diversity and equity. According to Hall, cultural aspects above the water constitute only a minuscule portion of the values making up the bigger picture beyond the surface.

- o The pyramid of hate is a tool to consider the results of establishing differences and prejudices amongst each other, which eventually leads to larger problems like genocide, illustrated by the prevalence of societal bias, hate, and oppression.

Pillar 4
INCLUSION

"Diversity without inclusion is simply a check in the box."

There is a reason the words "diversity" and "inclusion" usually appear together, so inclusion is the natural topic for this pillar. In this section, we will approach inclusion with consideration of parents and educators.

Chapter 7: Inclusion and Identity

What is inclusion?

While diversity, whether in the classroom, workplace, friend group, or organization, has numerous benefits, it can be hard to maintain. In large part, people perceived as "different" are often excluded from society or considered social outcasts. In some places and eras, this sort of exclusion has been explicit—such as India's caste system, or the United States' history of slavery and segregation. In other situations, it may not be so obvious, like unconscious bias in hiring practices or microaggressions. Regardless of scale or explicitness, those who are different or who deviate from the mainstream culture in some way often face marginalization and discrimination. Ensuring that groups and individuals have access to rights, opportunities, respect, and acceptance is crucial for a society. Being able to do this can transform the success and trajectories of communities and individuals.

In practice, inclusion can take various forms. Easy examples could be times, as a young person, that we felt left out in conversations and a friend brought us in with a smile and a question. In recent years, many media companies and political groups have answered to demands for increased representation which has led to minority groups seeing more accurate representations of their communities in areas from film to politics. Other examples of diversity and inclusion practices include commitments, from employers or schools, to diversifying candidate pools and maintaining certain levels of representation.

Can we then conclude that inclusivity is a direct product of equal access to opportunities and resources for people who might feel excluded or marginalized otherwise? Just like we had discussed above, those with physical or mental disabilities and ones originating from minority groups are most at risk of social division and hierarchy, and when a society comes together to make them feel otherwise, it then defines its utmost success as a community.

If you really followed the book as it had called out to be, you would remember the earlier chapters mentioning culture as a practice of bringing different ethnicities together in a universe that starts to look like a patchwork quilt of sorts, with contrasting people and lifestyles amalgamating together into a unique capsule.

Digital workspaces, an illustration

Since equity, equality, and inclusivity are social aspects very intricately linked together, let us change the classroom dynamic a bit to get a better idea. It would be absurd to not mention how the mass global coronavirus pandemic shifted the complete setup of classrooms worldwide, where, I am sure, the introverts thanked dear Lord for putting them out of the misery of human interaction, while most of the rest of us felt limited to just communicating with the walls. What might seem even hilarious to you, is that some schools expected the kids to dress up to sit behind laptops and talk to the walls. I mean, to think of the audacity!

Be it office spaces or schools, people have learned to live with the new set of conditions, where they have no other choice but to take to their homes to "shelter in." A few office goers might hold the opinion that it only makes life easier for them in the sense that they do not need to worry about dressing formal waist down, simply because unless their toddler walks in and knocks the laptop down, what are the chances of anyone knowing they are only wearing a pair of polka-dot boxers beneath the suit and tie? Working from home might deceivingly look like a privilege, in that you might not have to opt for the higher-risk options. Even those attending school might find it easier to doze off, especially if the cameras are turned off, or pretend their bad Wi-Fi is not getting the sound across when the instructor calls out their name, you know the drill. Some even go as far as having an entire conversation pretending to fake a connection lag while talking, so that they get a better time to think over the questions asked. For people who shy away from public speaking and like confined alone spaces just because it is their personality trait, online learning is much more effective.

However, the reason it is categorized as deceiving or misleading is that power struggle can lead to an unfair deal of marginalization in the school and workforce. Some get the chance to speak more than the marginalized voices and perspectives, which get buried deep into the ground. Many workers exploring their field of work have admitted that the notion to conduct rare online meetings with the intention of bringing attention to a face-to-face interaction no longer exists.

Now, the frightening and most concerning thing is that the end in line is the meeting itself and all experience and info that gets shared there is the final version of how things get expected to play out eventually is also final and absolute. It gets particularly hard, besides just maintaining decorum and productivity, to stay functional and operational while working at home, especially if you have a whole clan of rascals as kids. You must have gotten the chance to see several awkward, embarrassing situations created when someone's infant just barges into the room uncalled for, announcing they need a diaper change.

Another lesson that online tutoring and working have taught us is that some things have remained the same, such as staying indoors to work or the skepticism of medical institutions. However, what may have changed is the shrinking rift between the disabled and abled, as we have come to realize several workplace accommodations and worker protections that were missing before the workplace. Can we then say that building a new reality together centered around a pandemic has ultimately brought us closer together as individuals? Is human survival then strongly reliant on critical connections over the internet to create a sense of better inclusivity, or have our online platforms also, to some degree, failed in filling the void of unjust practice? Since the decisions organizations make online have started to become an integral product of online interaction, it is vital for participants to engage and include one another by giving everyone a fair chance to speak.

A great shout out to those brands going over and above to make their surroundings more inclusive and to help create better striving, equitable, and accessible online platforms where diversity is welcome and not looked down upon. So, if you work at a place where trainers, designers, and capacity builders feel free to share their tips and tricks to motivate others, and where achievement is a combined approach, you should really consider yourself lucky. Perhaps when we read and understand human interaction as a conversation, it is easy for the mind to make sense rather than understanding comprehensive perspectives and approaches.

Evaluation of inclusivity over time

When you ask organizers their views on the "hierarchy of voices" in terms of who gets to speak most, you would feel surprised at how their consensus points towards virtual meetings explicitly where they only get to see a "few voices privileged over the rest."

Put your hand up if you have ever attended a meeting and have so much to say but feel like those two know-it-alls at the front seat gain all the limelight. Put another hand up if you feel you do not feel secure and empowered enough when you express your thoughts over something as if your opinions seem meaningless, weightless to everyone else around. Some people can even come off as pretentious or dominant because of the diverse skill set they try to show off and put up a facade about. When the quieter ones do not see the others respecting the rules of the workplace or classroom where children must raise a hand to speak, they feel their voice will not reach the other end of the class and that would lead to more embarrassment. Someone out there actually has weak connections, so they might already find it hard to pay attention.

However, such cycles, when left ignored, keep replaying in a loop and can leave you feeling stranded. If you wish to find joy in your life as a parent, you must seek it from within yourself, it is there, just a bit stubborn to come out is all. One way of subverting such interfering thoughts to disrupt our perceptions of the world and the relationships that flow with it is self-talk to remind yourself that we are never helpless or alone in situations like these. It is our mind who makes us believe otherwise while it is us as individual human beings who have a stronghold in deciding to design, hold, and manage a space, and make it as inclusive as we wish to see it.

When we combine perceptions and assumptions of the mannerisms establishing power and authority within a single social space, we then come to compare it to the reasons why they feel such a privilege and how it gets expressed.

Some people take precedence over others in terms of their ability to hold their own or get the chance to speak more since they are better set than others. This can mean that they are more talented or capable in one department as opposed to the other members, but this exaggerated difference results in a heightened and a very unnecessary hierarchy because it gets left unattended. So how do folks consume greater lengths of power and privilege in virtual spaces than others? Some might possess the resources that give them a better way to access hardware and software. For instance, a mother with a child at home might not be able to fully commit to the nine to five vigorous job hours and that affects her space in the organization. She might start to feel less included in the meetings, feeling like she is steering far away from the company demographics.

An ongoing systematic privilege exists for those who have all the needed technology at home, such as a workplace setup or personal computer. The extra cherry on top is for those who have the latest version of the meeting platform and contain the authority of linking the virtual meeting, already establishing their place in the system. Those conducting business phone calls over the phone are different from those using desktop applications a handicapped. The benefits of using a faster processor are that you can chat and conduct business dealings easily, not just at the workplace, and also use applications like Google Classrooms to hasten uploading assignments as well.

Digital literacy is another factor that can set one apart from the others because, while it is integral to make full use of access to computers, it is also essential to realize that not everyone can have a fundamental digital experience. Not everyone can type at the speed of light, or find their way through a computer interface, or a virtual meeting.

Now comes something most of us, unfortunately, exercise hardly any control over, but something that holds incredible power in terms of defining your significance and contribution to an industry you wish to strive in. Some of you might have already guessed I am talking about good internet bandwidth. This might sound like a cliche advertisement to you right now, or one of those cheesy extracts from a magazine for parenting, but better physical connections strengthen emotional conditions as well. Therefore, an employee with better connection quality would play clearer videos and voiceovers on most virtual meeting platforms, which helps in creating a positive image.

Privilege can also take the face of a person who works better in a quieter, well-lit place where they have a good office set up and enough privacy to work in peace. A person like this naturally has an upper hand over his counterparts who might find it harder to keep up online.

Although the digitalized world has brought with it several advantages, it comes with a fair share of inclusivity. Many websites do not cater to the neurodivergent needs of those with disabilities, who are hard of hearing and of sight. This makes me think and believe just how much the world still needs to progress to make it a place more acceptable and sensitive to the needs of everyone. Our efforts in finishing off hierarchies start and end with gender, and even that has so much left to work on. While reading the extract also I was surprised to know that the connection between online social platforms and disability is such a rare phenomenon that it did not even click at first.

When we talk about the concept of freedom in a patriarchal society, we often miss put on the glaring, most important, and dangerous outcome of power dynamics, where a group of individuals does not get heard and seen the way they deserve to be because of being hampered by something that often is not even under their control. And that, my friends, is one of the most tragic mysteries of society. Care-taking roles, especially for elders or children, should never get made to look like a hassle or a barricade affecting your performance at work. The same goes for language. If extensive brands cannot take the pains to plug in subtitles for their ethnically diverse clientele, then what does that have to say about it? Is it their way of justifying that language can be used as an excuse to hold people against their inability to understand linguistics apart from their own? As horrific as this may sound to you now, it is a concept especially prevalent in places where the host culture and identity of a particular goes over and beyond the inclusivity and fair integration of society.

Power hierarchies and their effect on inclusivity

An unfair distribution of such hierarchies can take several ugly forms, even in a virtual meeting without the usual in-person interaction. A group of people takes it upon themselves to speak on every comment possible and that overshadows the presence of others. A perpetual interruption of comments of others which deliberately disrupts dialog. Not taking into consideration what others think and say and always restricting their debate to their own lives. They might even use unnecessary jargon and acronyms that not everybody would comprehend.

Think of it this way: You just got transferred to an American schooling system from the one you followed in Turkey, and suddenly you find people using even trickier words than the simpler ones you already found challenging to wrap your head around. Listening to them converse or debate is like a layperson overhearing a conversation between two doctors deciding which form of fissure they would need to go for before a complex procedure.

Having a rough consensus with the approach of "this is how we will do this" opinion, disregarding others' opinions, is another damaging form of privilege that can create inclusivity at great length. At times, the particularly problematic ones, while knowing full well of the intention behind what another person in the class meant, still choose to pick on them by paraphrasing and re-framing their comments in a way that disrespects the original meaning of whatever was said. Last but the most demeaning of all, are those blatant offensive comments and passive-aggressive eye rolls that can make anyone feel like they do not belong, that they come with too many patchworks on their quilts from the ocean full of lifetime experiences accompanied by a feeling of hopelessness that no matter what to do, they will always be the fish out of water. The fish sitting at the brink of a boat, not fully submerged but also barely alive. And that is something we must protect our children from so they may never come to see such a day.

In conclusion, when we convince our kids of the power of their voice and ability in speaking out, we must make them feel loved and appreciated for whatever they have in store for us. If they do not come to their parents and teachers with their creative, speculative minds, where else would they go?

Key reflections

- o Regardless of scale or explicitness, those who are different or who deviate from the mainstream culture in some way often face marginalization and discrimination.

- o Ensuring that groups and individuals have access to rights, opportunities, respect, and acceptance is crucial for a society. Being able to do this can transform the success and trajectories of communities and individuals.

o When we combine perceptions and assumptions of the mannerisms establishing power and authority within a single social space, we then come to compare it to the reasons why they feel such a privilege and how it gets expressed.

Chapter 8: Why Inclusion Matters for Children

Inclusiveness shouldn't be restricted to a specific group. Maybe the quiet introverted kid can add more to the on-going conversation than the constantly talking extroverted kid...Maybe all they need is a bit of motivation and the feeling of being included. To make things better you can even tell the extroverted kid to wait for their turn to speak. This will allow everyone to express their opinions. Inclusivity is not about getting the oppressed out of their misery by taking down people who are already at the top, it is about giving everyone equal opportunity to be at the top, to grow and to learn. You don't tell the extroverted kid to shut up when trying to make the introverted kid talk, you put the introverted kid in a position where it is easier for them to talk.

As a teen, remember the last time someone in your friend group was too quiet during a conversation. Did you try to talk them in? As a teacher, did you try to encourage the quiet kid to ask questions? As a parent, did you teach your children to be inclusive regardless of culture, race, or nationality? What goes around comes around. If your children show more openness and try to be inclusive, they will receive the same treatment. Kids learn from parents so before teaching your children to be inclusive you should try doing it yourself. Start by the way you treat other people and be a good role model. These kids will become parents tomorrow and what you teach them they will preach to their own children. This is why children are the base of society. You want to make a big change, start with the children.

Why should parents care about inclusion?

As stated earlier, parents play a key role in introducing major changes to society. Teachers are also included in this list of change makers, but since children spend more time at home with their parents, they are likely to pick up habits from them. Children should be taught to be inclusive from a young age because it is easier for children to adopt and act on things when they are young. When they reach their teen years, it becomes difficult to implant new ideas or replace old ideas with new ones. Moreover, teens usually spend more time with their friends or on the internet so they would most likely develop their mindset from those instead of their parents. This does not mean that once your child reaches teen age they are doomed and can never learn anything from you again. What this means is that it is harder to convince teens of something than to convince -let's say, an 8-year-old. Our actions reflect our mindset. So, if your children have a positive mindset, their actions will be positive as well.

Parents need to understand that exclusion is not something that only differently abled or minority children feel. Their so-called "normal" child can also be facing exclusion in the classroom or even at the playground. They may be afraid to join others due to the feeling of not being good enough. These seemingly "normal" children are often ignored since everyone just assumes that you have to be different to face exclusion. It does not even have to be physical, or action based. Exclusion can also occur due to differences in the way of thinking. Not every child is the same and so they all think differently. Parents should teach their children to be more accepting of these differences.

Teaching your children about inclusion teaches them a lot about respect and how to view others equally. It teaches them friendship and to accept differences, to look past the physical self. All of this will reflect in their children as well creating a generational difference. It also makes your children respect other cultures and learn something new. Parents should teach their children that inclusivity is not just for a few "special" children. All children deserve to be included, mainly in the classroom environment. Every student should have an equal opportunity to learn and to be able to ask questions. Choosing to not ask questions is another matter but creating an atmosphere where it is easier for everyone to be involved should be our priority. The way we approach inclusion also matters a lot since not every child can be treated the same way.

Encouraging inclusivity for special needs children

Even though everyone might agree on the importance of inclusion in a classroom, only a few can come up with effective plans to achieve this goal. This is not just a simple problem, it is complex. On the one hand, you want to teach special needs children in a regular classroom but, on the other hand, that may disrupt the flow of learning for other students which would be unfair to them. However, if you try to create a dedicated classroom for special needs children it might take things a bit slower than the regular classroom meaning that these kids would technically fall behind other kids. Moreover, a dedicated classroom would mean that these children would miss out on the traditional classroom experience.

So, what is the best solution? Some schools try to merge both classrooms together which gives special needs children an opportunity to enjoy the traditional classroom setting all the while making regular students aware of how special needs children learn. This provides a middle ground solution that seems to solve the problem; however, it also has its own complications. One of the biggest ones is competition. When you merge special needs children with regular children you are making them compete. Even though a child with special needs might be able to compete with a regular classmate with the right guidance, when talking about overall performance, regular children perform much better in the classroom than let's say children with autism. The difference is not that great however it can create a performance gap which may lead to a divide between students.

An alternative would be a dedicated classroom or a department for special needs children. This takes us to the slower pace problem, but if we can teach these children the same topics that are being taught in the traditional classroom but with a slightly lesser degree of complexity, these children might be able to compete with other normal students. Again, with the right guidance this performance gap can be greatly minimized but that also varies from one child to another. So, when trying to be inclusive we have to consider the classroom as a whole. Creating a separate profile for each child can be helpful since it would allow the teacher to work on specific requirements for each of their children. One of the biggest advantages of having a dedicated special needs department is that the staff will be fully trained to interact with these children. Moreover, the teachers can customize the classroom according to the needs of the students creating a better learning environment.

This shouldn't just be a classroom problem. Inclusivity needs to be embedded in society. We need to create a society where you do not have to worry about being careful around differently abled kids. I've seen people holding their kids back from saying anything around special needs children fearing that they might ask some embarrassing question. This thought process is justified to some extent because the main intent is to not offend the other person, but this will only create a wider gap. When parents act strangely around such children, it will send a negative message to their own kids. Instead of stopping your kid from asking questions, why not teach them to behave appropriately around their special needs friends. If your six-year-old son asks you why the neighbor's kid Kyle is missing an eye, you tell him why. Maybe he will not understand it just now, but it will still give him an answer. Shutting his question down will only feed his curiosity.

Encourage your children to spend time with differently abled kids. They will get to know them better and maybe even help them in the playground. Let them know that having a disability does not make these children any less deserving or any less good. As a society our goal should be to look at these children and not see any difference. Parents don't make much of an effort to introduce their children to special needs kids since they think that these kids do not have much to offer. These "special kids" may teach your child more than typical kids. This does not mean that your children should only be friends with differently abled kids, it just means to try and keep their friend circle diverse so they can broaden their perspective. Filling in your kids with inclusivity early in their lives will mean that by the time they turn fourteen, they will have no problem inviting a special needs friend to their birthday party or an outing. From a household level this might not seem like that big of a change but over an extended period this small change can convert into a societal norm.

Inclusion is not one size-fits-all

We have established by now that not every child is the same. There is a difference in the way you approach a shy child or an introvert though both have trouble speaking to people. The former needs encouragement while the latter needs a friendlier environment. To a stranger, both look the same since they both "don't talk" but their reason for not talking is different hence we must apply different tactics to solve it. Same is the case with inclusion. There is a difference in the way you would treat a handicapped kid and an autistic kid. Both need assistance, but in a different way.

There are also immigrant children who do not have any problem learning in the classroom, but they would still struggle to fit in with the rest of the class. They might also have a hard time making friends due to the cultural barrier. This can make them less interactive and minimize their creative abilities. To prevent this, students should be made to appreciate different cultures and learn from them. Celebrating different cultural days is a good way of spreading awareness. It also teaches students about history and how people live in different countries.

Teachers should try and analyze what works the best for their own students. Do not just copy what some other school did. Document each student separately and work with their parents to create a separate profile for them. Try to identify their weaknesses and their strengths and work on those. This will not only create an inclusive classroom but a generation of children who can appreciate the differences and look past the barriers set by our own perception.

However, achieving inclusion is not that simple. Part of it is due to the fact that humans have genetic differences (even though it accounts for about 0.01% of our genetic makeup). These differences mean that not everyone can be treated the same way. You have to consider each person as a separate individual not as a group identity. We have already discussed how two kids -one of them being shy and the other being an introvert display the same behavior, but their problem needs different methods of solving. Inclusion is much closer to equity than equality because the end goal is achieving diversity and everyone getting what they deserve.

To understand this further let's take the example of a mixed classroom. The classroom consists of different students, each with their own unique personalities and ways of learning. Our goal is to make this class as inclusive as possible. Let's start with the testing system. Now if we try to implement a testing system where everyone would be asked to answer the same five questions it will not give us the same result for all students. Some of them will perform better than the others. Okay, so we can just include different categories to this test. These categories will allow children to choose from different difficulties and types of questions which results in a more diverse and inclusive testing system. After this, let's move towards the actual learning process and how the seating will be arranged for this classroom. The way you seat students has a sizable impact on their learning abilities. Students at the back are less likely to participate in classroom discussions compared to students at the front. This usually happens when students are seated according to the typical row seating arrangement. A better alternative would be a circular seating arrangement in which students form a semi-circle around the teacher's desk. This allows the students more room to participate in class discussions or ask questions since each student is relatively at the same distance from their teacher. Look, the classroom is already looking inclusive!

But wait, what about autistic kids or kids with ADHD? For it to be a truly inclusive class, we must include special needs kids too or kids with learning disabilities. Here we can make use of technology. For example, children who have trouble following up with the regular pace of the class may get recorded videos of lectures that they can watch in their free time. Teachers can even set up extra classes for these children outside regular study hours to help them stay in the race. Since we are also including special needs children our previously suggested seating arrangement will not work. We now have a much more diverse list of students. Some of them may have hearing difficulty or

ADHD. Letting them all sit at the same distance from the teacher will not be appropriate. We need to customize the seating arrangement while keeping in view the individual problems of each student. Most schools do not care much about seating arrangements and students are allowed to sit wherever they want but when we have a diverse class like this, we need to keep everything in check. In fact, seating arrangements can have a fundamental impact on the learning abilities of certain students.

Niliam Shinde explained this pretty well in a discussion about seating plans in the classroom (Shinde, 2017) She stressed upon the need for introducing customized seating plans for special needs students. For example, a student with hearing disability should be seated in the front so it is easier for them to listen to the teacher. Similarly, students with ADHD shouldn't be seated too far away from the desk or near windows as it might lead to them getting distracted. Kids with learning disabilities or any physical disability for that matter should get more attention in the class since these children have a higher risk of becoming dropouts. Moreover, teachers should be trained to manage special needs children along with neurotypical children so that a peaceful classroom environment can be maintained.

Profiling each student individually is also important since it will allow for a better understanding of their problems. (Shinde, 2017).

All of this would be useless if the students are not taught to be inclusive themselves. This is where teachers as well as parents come in. When typical students start watching their minority or disabled peers as equals, we automatically achieve inclusion. Inclusion is not just about learning; it is about how we think. It is not about a group of students with disabilities or who feel left alone, it is about all of us. It is about society and how we treat people. This classroom is just a simple example, and we haven't even touched the tip of the iceberg. However, it does help us understand why inclusion is so complex. This complexity does not discard its importance. We need inclusion, our children need inclusion and society needs inclusion.

Diversity is something natural, but it cannot survive without inclusion. As a workplace becomes more inclusive it is diversity increases. This creates a better work environment which ultimately benefits the whole company. It is the same with society. If diversity is celebrated people feel more welcomed and start appreciating each other's differ-ences. It leads to the creation of a society where everyone is treated the same and has equal opportunities to prosper.

Key reflections

- o Inclusivity benefits everyone, not just select groups. Parents should teach their children that in-clusivity is not just for a few "special" children.

- o Inclusivity can transform on many levels, from family to school to workplaces to communities.

- o Teaching children about inclusion teaches them a lot about respect and how to view others equally. It teaches them friendship and to accept differences, to look past the physical self.

- o All children deserve to be included, mainly in the classroom environment. Every student should have an equal opportunity to learn and to be able to ask questions.

Chapter 9: Educational Inclusion Case Study

This scenario study involves the effect of providing appropriate intervention support with a student with dyslexia and the journey that his family went through to ensure that he was taught appropriately in a variety of settings. The story begins in North Carolina, when a student that we will call Eli was about 18 months old. Eli was then the second child that the married couple had, and they noticed that he wasn't talking as quickly as their first child and that his articulation and language skills seemed delayed. The family sought out outside support through an organization called The Child Development Services Agency. After formal assessments, it was determined that the child had a moderate speech delay. So, an IEP (individual education plan) was created to provide speech therapy through local organizations and outside practitioners that often came to the family's home.

When Eli entered kindergarten, he wasn't reading and his mother, a teacher at his school became concerned. After speaking with the regular classroom teacher, she was assured that all was well. Eli's Mom wasn't satisfied and took the student out of a regular brick and mortar setting the following year and enrolled him into a virtual setting, where he could receive more 1:1 support with learning at home with his mom and brother. During that time, Eli was given his first IEP that was supposed to address deficits in reading and math. During Eli's second grade year, he returned to a regular brick and mortar setting and still was significantly behind in reading, but definitely caught on faster to math. Finally, during the third- grade year, his parents decided to figure out exactly what was going and sought outside educational testing, which revealed that Eli was dyslexic.

During his third-grade year, the information was shared with the student's local school, and they began to consider ways to provide more appropriate instruction for Eli. During his fourth-grade year, his parents decided to completely remove him from the public setting and enroll him into a home school and part-day private school to address his unique learning profile, not completely reassured that the current school would be able to meet his needs and propel him forward academically.

During the time that Eli was in homeschool and a part day private school that focused on meeting the needs of students with dyslexia and ADHD, his mother got training in a program called Orton Gillingham to teach Eli at home. The next three years would be a turning point for Eli, his family, and a newly created idea––The Catch-up Center. You see Eli's mom sincerely appreciated the $20,000 education that Eli received at the local private school, but felt that she could lower the cost, meet the needs of more families, and essentially more effectively meet the needs of Eli.

In 2017, she founded a nonprofit, The Catch-up Center, Inc. It was founded on the idea of changing the face of education in a way that meets the needs of all students, including those with learning differences. The Catch-up Center took the good parts of teaching and added their "secret sauce" to create a program that is affordable, virtual, and works well with the student's base school. Eli is now a student at The Catch-up Center, along with other students that are or were significantly behind in reading and math. His sense of achievement has skyrocketed as the center created a program designed to meet the needs of the whole child, specifically addressing areas of deficit that include low self-esteem, lack of motivation, and ineffective teaching practices that plagues schools today, as they try hard to meet the needs of a vast array of different learning profiles during a single school day.

Eli is currently achieving on grade level in math and steadily making progress in reading. He feels empowered to go his base school with newfound confidence in his ability and confidence in allowing his learning difference to work to his benefit, seeing the good parts of having dyslexia and embracing those good parts. You see, this family took a difficult situation and used it to make a difference in the world of education. Eli's mother is a woman of faith and realized early in the journey that the key to helping Eli was going to be helping other students that are just like Eli. The Catch-up Center changes lives and proves that there is no one size fits all approach to learning.

Key reflections

- o Eli's situation demonstrates a situation that many families and educator's encounter.

o Finding an appropriate education plan can transform a student's educational experience and the trajectory for their career or life in general.

Pillar 5:
BELONGING

A deep sense of love and belonging is an irreducible need of all people. We are biologically, cognitively, physically, and spiritually wired to love, to be loved, and to belong. When those needs are not met, we don't function as we were meant to. We break. We fall apart. We numb. We ache. We hurt others. We get sick.

Brené Brown

Chapter 10: When the Magic Happens

This chapter covers the topic of belonging with a discussion of the phenomenon as well as a case study for a meaningful illustration of belonging and exclusion in real life.

What is belonging?

When you are at your home there is a sense of safety, a sense of comfort and familiarity. Have you ever thought about where that feeling is coming from? It is not just because your home provides you shelter and a space to survive, it is more than that. It is the people, your family, your partner that makes you feel valued. These people make us feel needed and they make us feel like we have a role in the house. They allow us to be ourselves. Without these people, the same house will look empty and deserted. It becomes cold and lifeless.

Belonging is about fulfillment and being accepted. To belong means to be a part of something. It can even be people that you belong with. Most of us want to be accepted. We want to be valued and appreciated for the things we do and the things we can do. It is something fundamental to us humans. Some turn to religion while others look for communities just to feel that sense of belonging. Even then some people may feel left out. All because of that 0.01% difference in their genetic makeup. As a Cameroonian Immigrant who moved abroad, I have experienced all this firsthand. From being called the "Jamaican b**ch" while on my nursing job, to being told not to apply for a job because of my heavy accent. I have seen and felt it all. I kept looking for a place where I could find people like me.

For too long I struggled to be culturally aware. Only after leaving Canada and moving to Washington, DC, did I realize what I really wanted. I wasn't looking to meet people like me, I just wanted to find a place I could call home. A place where I could feel the sense of belonging. This was the turning point of my life, and I became aware of the importance of appreciating cultural differences. I applied for a job at a hospital in Delaware even after a stranger warned me "I wouldn't bother applying there, they are racists and won't offer you a position. Plus, you're an immigrant with a heavy accent and a black woman." This same hospital is where I found my home and the sense of belonging I was looking for! All of that changed my perspective on life, and I came to realize why a sense of belonging is so important to people. Nothing feels worse than being left out, or being treated like you don't matter.

Why identity matters

Humans are afraid of being alone. After all, we are social animals. From the time we were out hunting with sticks to the present day, people still want to be associated with something or someone. This association and belonging helps us move forward in life. It makes us much more creative and efficient at work. You wouldn't put much effort into work if you didn't feel like you belonged in that workplace, would you? The same is true for large communities. When society as a whole comes together, it is important to make sure everyone feels welcomed and loved. Societies that discriminate and do not promote inclusion fail to progress. A society does not just consist of a single group of people. It contains different groups with different cultural values and capabilities all of which are equally needed for the society to function properly. The sense of belonging helps people find meaning in their lives. It makes them feel worthwhile and at home.

Most often people are not fortunate enough to find a workplace which they can call their home. It mostly happens with people who are deemed different. It can be due to a difference of color, birthplace, culture or even physical capabilities. Having these differences does not make these people any less human. They can add the same value to society as every other person. All they need to show their true potential is love and the sense of belonging. Immigrant students who have trouble adapting to the cultural differences in their new school often end up without making any friends. This leads them to a path of loneliness and lack of passion. The same happens to kids having disabilities. In schools where inclusion is not taken seriously, students who are left out often end up becoming dropouts. The feeling of being accepted and valued can help these students cope with the hardships they may feel at school. It's all about embracing those differences and appreciating different cultures.

Identity and the sense of belonging

The way I like to define identity is how we see and display ourselves. Our beliefs, our morals, our likes and dislikes are all part of our identity. In simple terms, it's who we are. Identity and belonging are closely related. To be yourself you need to have that sense of belonging and acceptance. Identity is not something concrete and can change fluently. In fact, every little experience that you have is changing or in other words shaping your identity. Every person holds this identity sacred. You cannot achieve your true potential unless you are true to your identity and to yourself. This means that the only way to unlock your full potential is being yourself and to be ourselves, we need to feel acknowledged and accepted. This is where both terms combine.

People may even alter their own identity just to get accepted or cherished. For example, if you are sitting with a group of people who don't like football you may try to start a conversation with them by pretending to not like football. In this example you are changing your own identity in order to get accepted into this group and feel that sense of belonging. Our identity isn't the result of a single entity, but rather, it is a combination of almost everything that is happening in our life and around us. It reflects who we are and what we believe in. However not everyone sees you the same way as your own perception of self. Our image of identity is formed by the combination of our actions and our beliefs but to other people the only thing visible is how we look and how we act. The only reliable sources of information available to them are our actions and our physical self. Therefore, their perception of us is made according to those factors. This is also known as social identity.

Creating belonging

Identity can be influenced by almost everything. Your habits, your friends, your family, how you treat others, where you live and so on. On the other hand, belonging requires commonality and acceptance. The biggest impact on a person's identity comes from where they live. The country of birth has a huge significance in determining a person's identity since it is where they would spend most part of their life. Similarly, place of living and family also affects our identity. It is where we get our culture from.

While identity is something that is constructed without any conscious effort, the sense of belonging requires you to put in the work. If you want to be accepted by a group, you must first talk to them and convince them that you actually deserve to be in that group. People are often hesitant to include someone who they think is different. That is mostly due to a lack of understanding, but it also has a lot to do with our brain functioning. We don't like change. It makes us feel insecure and unsafe. Looking at the same thing all day might be boring, but it is still predictable. Change is unpredictable and that's why people have trouble welcoming others who look different. Of course, this does not justify treating them unfairly just because they are different. After all, no two people are the same in this world.

We try to use skin color and nationality as an excuse to deem someone to be different. Once a person is labeled as being the "other" it becomes easier to zone them out of all activities. This puts our identity at risk. These labels dictate the general perception of a particular group and to avoid being labeled people will often try to change who they are and blend in with the crowd. All this does is create a fake persona that might make them feel a sense of belonging, but it takes away something much more important, their true identity.

Belonging vs. diversity and inclusion

Belonging is closely related to inclusion. When a society becomes more inclusive, more people feel welcomed and accepted. No one has to put on a fake mask in order to blend in. They can just be themselves and still enjoy equal opportunities. In a society like this people are taught to appreciate differences because that's what makes us unique. These differences give rise to the creativity of humans. Imagine how boring the world would be if we all looked and acted the same! To create a sense of belonging we need to appreciate people for who they are and how they are.

Becoming culturally aware is a big part of promoting inclusion. There should be a human-to-human link between people instead of a cultural or geographical link. The people who often feel lost and alone include minorities or immigrants who are looking for a place to call their home. These people belong to different cultures hence they have trouble getting along with the locals. We need to help these minority or immigrant groups by making them feel accepted and at home.

The sense of belonging is as important to humans as all other basic needs. A person may be able to survive alone but they may not be able to live with the feeling of *being* alone. Celebrating diverse cultures and spending time with people from different races and ethnicities creates understanding about these cultures and people. Teach your kids to diversify their friend group by not restricting themselves to a single group or culture. Practice inclusion yourself and try to spend your time with disabled and minority members of society. Encourage your children from a young age to invite their friend with special needs to their birthday parties so they don't feel left out.

Belonging and inclusion are related, but they are not the same thing. Some people even confuse diversity with belonging and inclusion. All three of these terms have different meanings but they are all somehow connected. Diversity is a natural occurrence and is something which has been embedded in our DNA. Geographical and cultural differences also create diversity among humans. As societies get more diverse, inclusion becomes more important. When people from different ethnicities and cultures are living together, it is important that all of them have equal access to opportunities. In order for a society to prosper, all of its communities need to also prosper.

We have already discussed in the previous chapter that inclusion cannot be achieved by bringing down some people and lifting others. So, diversity is different cultures and people from different backgrounds living together while inclusion is letting each of them have equal opportunities and equal rights. In other words, inclusion means to not let them feel any different. The feeling people get when they are included or accepted is called belonging. You can see how each term is different yet so connected. Belonging is a feeling while inclusion is a behavior. Diversity on the other hand is nature.

Relationships, environment, and the identity and sense of belonging

Relationships have a sizable role in sculpting a person's identity or at least their social identity. To be with people and to get close to them, most of us change our identities. We morph into something more likable and something that is easier to accept. Belonging is not just about acceptance. It is about accepting people for who they are and what they can become. If you must let go of your true identity in order to feel accepted, that is not where you belong. You belong where you and your capabilities are valued. The closest we can get to this feeling is when we are with our family or close friends. They make us feel complete and valued. You do not create a fake persona at home. That is because everyone accepts you for who you are. Even then it is impossible for people to recognize your true identity. No one other than you know who you really are.

Relationships make us feel strong. When we are in a relationship, we become more comfortable with our true identity. Relationships are important in finding one's sense of belonging. It does not always work out though. Sometimes, people judge you for your social identity and when your true identity is finally revealed, they have trouble accepting it. It is good to change but never to lose your true self. You do not belong with someone who wants you to change for them. Your goal in a relationship should be finding your identity and not changing it. Apart from relationships, our environment also affects our identity. For example, people who have spent more time abroad than in their native country will identify with that foreign country.

The ever-changing behavior of our identity makes it so difficult to understand. Belonging on the other hand, does not change with the environment. It changes with the people. It depends on who we spend time with and who accepts us for our true identity. In order to discover our true identity, we need to be in an environment where we feel a sense of belonging. In other words, we need to be with people who make us feel needed and accepted (Mind Metaphors, n.d).

Why should we care? What is the impact of this on our lives and identity?

The sense of belonging impacts our lives in a lot of ways. It gives us a reason to live and a purpose in life. It helps to create bonds with people. The people we belong with are the ones we value the most. Even to the point where we start feeling their joy and sorrow. Belonging is such an incredible feeling. Having friends in school who value your differences and uniqueness can make your classroom feel like home. It helps you cope with stress and the downs of life. On a broader level it helps create a stronger bond between communities. On a personal level, not feeling valued or accepted can cause depression and anxiety. It prevents individuals from exploring their skills and expertise because they feel worthless.

Individuals who grow up in families where they do not feel that sense of belonging often end up having a negative view of the whole world. This is extremely wrong since it can actually take away their ability to trust other people. They may not be able to bond with other people or form any lasting relationships. With all these challenges it will be hard for them to add anything of value to society. All of those years of being alienated can cause them to embed it into their own identity.

Why is the feeling of belonging important and how can it be created in your own life or for others in society?

It is the duty of parents to make their children feel accepted and appreciated. Spending time with your children is very important. Some parents spend too much time focusing on their job that they forget to spend time with their children. Do not spend too much time away from your children, especially during their early days of growth. It is the time when children are beginning to develop their identity and mindset. Neglecting your children during this time period can lead to them feeling unappreciated and devalued. Parents are the first teachers for their children and most children often consider their parents to be their role models. So before teaching anything to your children make sure that you are practicing it as well. Act on what you preach and try to be a good role model for your children.

Teachers can help students feel the sense of belonging by making the classroom inclusive. Students should be taught to help their fellow disabled peers and to value each other's perspectives and way of thinking. The best thing a teacher can do is to create a classroom full of students who have the ability to see past each other's skin colors or heritage, students who can help others discover their identities and students who are open to accepting change and different cultures.

Case study: Tawonga Msowoya

Tawonga's story reminds me of my own, which is why I've included it here. We both left our countries in search of belonging elsewhere. Whoever we are, and wherever we come from, we are all human and have many of the same needs. One important aspect of these needs is belonging and being treated with respect; it is something we all crave throughout our human experience. But sometimes, we are rejected by the people in our own circles, whether that is our ethnic group, our religion, or another community. The people we expect to embrace us will sometimes be the ones who reject us. Treating one another with respect and dignity, especially those in our close circles, is something I believe we should encourage. My experience––and Tawonga's described below––remind me how important it is to remember that our difference and our experiences make us a cultural add, not a cultural fit.

> "I was born to a middle-class family in Malawi, a small country in Southern Africa. When I was 7, my parents placed me in one of the country's top private schools alongside the children of political figures, business moguls and expatriates. From my first days, I knew I was unlike the rest. I often felt out of place and gravitated towards children who shared my skin color. But even there, I felt my prior life experiences and age made me evidently different, even though many came down to small and subtle differences.

I felt embarrassed by the things that made me different and I bent and molded myself in my mission to assimilate and to belong to the dominant (White) culture. My speech took on a slight twang and my name mutated to accommodate foreign ears. I drifted further away from what made me Malawian, clinging occasionally to the language, speaking it with peers and family. My efforts to assimilate left me more disconnected; the identity I worked so hard to fabricate left me untethered, straddling the line between two cultures.

My way to my identity started with books—a novel by an African author left me thirsting for more stories featuring people like me. Pan Africanism and my heritage influenced me. I changed how I dressed, the stories and anecdotes I used to define my life, and I suddenly felt pride in my peoples' languages, the regions' kaleidoscope of cultural, and a new sense of connection with extended family. I finally began to feel like I belonged.

I also discovered my passion, becoming involved in activism with a focus on women's rights. I had always felt my position denied me freedoms that my brothers could claim, but now this realization was armed with an understanding of the forces and systemic "isms" that shape our reality. The louder my voice got, the more I referred to the past and, ironically, the more I could access spaces I initially tried to evolve myself to occupy.

My journey of finding my identity and belonging is one I am sure others can relate to. That young, 7-year-old girl became a Mandela Washington Fellow, and in my younger years, I may have found myself among those who left the continent and never came back. As a confident 25-year-old activist and feminist, my visit to the US had me asking "What could Africa do for the US?" My 6-week experience in the US was less about the nation's greatness and more about how my identity––that I had fought so hard to shed all those years ago––is the very thing that makes me stand out and thrive in that environment."

(Originally written by Tawonga Kwangu Msowoya, edited for length.)

From Cameroon and Malawi, Tawonga and I made our ways to the United States, where we eventually met. Now, we have the honor of sharing our stories––with confidence and pride for our respective cultures. At some point in our journeys, we both felt lost somewhere along the way and discovered that our identity and sense of belonging could not be found solely in our external circumstances or validation from others. Although it took time, trial and error (and certainly an emotional toll), we connected to ourselves and our cultural heritages, which gave us a sense of self-security, wellbeing, and self-confidence––something we didn't have when we tried to hide and repress our identities out of shame. It is difficult to resist pressures to fit yourself into the mold created by others, but the results of doing so are transformative.

Key reflections

- o Belonging is about fulfillment and being accepted. To belong means to be a part of something.

- o To discover our true identity, we need to be in an environment where we feel a sense of belonging. In other words, we need to be with people who make us feel needed and accepted.

- o Teachers and parents can help young people feel a sense of belonging either at home or in the classroom. Parents and educators should be sure to lead by example and to "practice what you preach."

Chapter 11: Guide for Parents

Parents often keep their kids in the dark about things like culture and diversity. They don't feel the need to describe these concepts to their children; not because they don't believe in them, but because they don't think learning about all of these things is important for their children. The truth is, if you do not educate your children on topics like the importance of inclusion or identity from a young age, it might become difficult to plant these ideas in their minds later on. Once a kid becomes a teen, they have trouble adapting to different ideas. This chapter is a guide to all of those parents who do not know how to go about teaching these concepts.

Acknowledging differences

The first step is acknowledging differences. It is a fact that all humans are different. Teach your children that it is okay to have differences. Not everyone has to dress or look a certain way to get accepted into society. We all are unique, be it our skin color or our physical capabilities. The important thing is that we recognize these differences and accept them as part of our identity. In order to bring a change in society, we have to first look inwards. Think about how you treat people who are different. When was the last time you invited or visited a minority or immigrant friend? Once you start practicing inclusion, your children will automatically adopt it too.

Encourage curiosity

Children are a bit curious, and this curiosity may lead to them exploring on their own. Don't shush your kids when they ask questions about disabled people or people of color. Teach them calmly and tell them why these people look different. Shutting down your kid will only lead to an increased curiosity. Moreover, encourage your kids to make their friends list diverse and get to know children from different cultures. This will help them a lot in understanding different cultures and traditions while creating a stronger bond with their friends.

Take some time off and teach your children about culture and identity. Try to make them feel valued and accepted. Do not discourage them when they are trying something new, instead try to help them so that they do not feel alone. Make your children feel a sense of belonging.

Confront discrimination

Never ignore discrimination. Whether it is at work, outside or even at your own house. Always treat people equally so that when your children grow up, they can also follow in your footsteps. One of the worst things you can teach your children is to ignore injustice and discrimination. If you ignore something your kids might think that it is normal.

Share your experience

Sharing your own experiences can be a powerful way to teach not just your children but people who are unaware of the importance of becoming culturally aware. It can give them a different perspective to look at and provide an opportunity to view things from a new light. Moreover, these experiences can also help your children act more appropriately towards others.

Familiarize yourself with your culture

Getting to know about your culture is very important. Most parents do not bother teaching their kids about their own culture. Teach your kids about culture but don't restrict their knowledge towards their own culture. Encourage them to explore other cultures as well. This will allow your children to respect and appreciate other cultures as well. Becoming culturally aware means that they will be able to get along with a diverse group of people and make them feel welcomed. Moreover, culture helps people in the search of identity. When people from a specific culture move abroad, they do not just move there alone, they also bring their culture with them. Allow your children to embrace their culture and language because this is what shapes our identity. Immigrant parents with children in the USA can provide opportunities to attend events and community gatherings with people from their home country for opportunities to learn about their culture and language. This might look like attending monthly tribal meetings, attending annual tribal conventions, communicating with family in the parents' country of birth, and getting to know the family's grandparents.

Embrace intercultural exchange and learning

Parents should be open to celebrating different holidays and traditions that promote inclusivity and a sense of belonging. These celebrations may not mean much to us but for some people it is a way to represent and promote their culture. These holidays and celebrations serve as a way of spreading cultural awareness and preserving these cultures. Teach your children about diverse cultures to create a sense of equity, inclusion and belonging.

Appreciate your child's talents

Every child is different and unique in their own way. This difference and uniqueness results in creativity and innovation therefore it should be valued and appreciated. Encourage your kids to showcase their true talents and capabilities. Teach them to use their differences as tools rather than obstacles in their way to success.

Practice attentiveness and active listening

Parents don't usually listen to their kids and what they say. They may pretend to be attentive but all they are doing is hearing them. Kids actually have a lot to say and paying attention to what they say can make them feel valued. I know it can get annoying at times when your kid keeps interrupting you in the middle of something important but all they are doing is asking for your attention. Even if you can't fully turn your focus towards what they are saying, just pretend to pay attention so they do not feel ignored.

Foster independence and responsibility

Encourage your child to make their own decisions and allow them to learn from their mistakes. To me failure is a far better teacher than anything else. Making their own decisions promotes a sense of responsibility in your children. They become more aware of the consequences of their actions and most importantly they learn to handle failure. If they have trouble doing something you can help them out but do not let your kids be dependent on you for long. It takes away their drive and sense of responsibility. Allow them to handle their own finances from an early age. You may still monitor what they do but let them figure it out their own way.

Emphasize kindness

Teach your children the importance of treating other people with kindness and respect irrespective of their skin color and ethnicity. This will make them learn how to create equity and make others feel inclusive and accepted. You should also encourage your children to learn about different cultures and increase their cultural awareness.

Encourage diversity in your child's friend groups and experiences

If your children have friends from different backgrounds, they may get to learn a lot. Having a diverse friend group will allow your kids to gain different insights about other cultures and traditions. They may even get to know what being different feels like. This will also teach them not to discriminate against anyone based on their looks or background. Make your children watch diverse media to make them understand what diversity is. Teach your children that it is our differences that make us interesting and unique. Let them know the importance of appreciating and accepting your differences as a part of your identity. These differences don't make anyone less or greater. It is only our capabilities and potential that sets us apart from others.

Avoid using disabilities and appearances as labels

Never label someone by their disability or appearance and teach your children to do the same. Labeling someone by their physical appearance restricts that person and their potential only to that label. With time these labels become a part of their social identity. When your children hear you use some label to mention your friend instead of their name, they start thinking that this is completely normal. When it actually is not. Try to be a good role model for your children and practice what you preach.

Hopefully, this chapter provided you with ideas and strategies for incorporating diversity and culture in your family life. This process is not a quick one, and learning and cultural experiences can be a lifelong journey. There also are not answers, strategies, or ideas that apply to every single family, so take the time to brainstorm and consider what will work best for you and your children.

Chapter 12: Guide for Educators

This section provides advice for educators in the form of teaching suggestions, reflections, and a lesson plan suggestion about efforts to a safe and inclusive learning environment.

Get to know your students

In order to create a better learning environment teachers and students should develop an understanding. Teachers should make a conscious effort in getting to know their students. This lets them see things from the perspective of students. However, don't push it too far since you also need to have that position of authority over your students. Try to be their friend and a teacher at the same time. An effective way of getting to know your students is by creating student profiles. You create a file and name each student in a list. In this list you write down their learning strengths, their weaknesses, their likes/dislikes and everything that you think might be helpful to you in making them learn better. Profiling also helps provide close attention to each student. Not every student may require one to one attention, but it can be implemented for those students who are having trouble learning in the class.

Address inequality

Unfortunately, inequality in education is a reality. It starts at the top of the education system down to the classrooms. It is upon the teacher to make sure none of their students ever receive unjust treatment. If they stand against inequality their students will also learn the same. Avoid favoritism in the classroom and make sure every student has equal opportunity to learn and to progress. When possible, check-in with students about their access to internet and digital resources. If their circumstances make digital or online learning difficult or impossible, consider alternative strategies so they do not fall behind. Take strong actions against bullying and look out for students who might show signs of mental distress. A lot of students who face bullying never share it with anyone due to embarrassment. So, make it easier for students to address such issues with you and try to garner their trust. Inequality in the classroom can lead to discrimination and there should be no room for discrimination in education.

Use language that promotes positivity and does not reinforce existing stereotypes

Language can have a huge impact on other people and how they see you. Try to use polite and formal language when talking to students. Call them out by their name even when you are mentioning them to someone else. If any student has a physical disability, try not to mention it in a negative or undermining way but let them see it as a strength. Labeling students into a particular category is always wrong no matter what your intent is. I have seen teachers call their students troublesome or "usual suspects." This type of labeling is wrong since it can stick with the student and make it harder for them to change. Instead of using these labels try to encourage them into doing something good and call them out by their real names. Discourage stereotyping students based on their skin color or background. Teach your students that everyone is different and looks have nothing to do with a person's achievements.

Connect with your student's families and communities

Another important step in getting to know your students is connecting with their families and communities. It teaches you about their way of life and their culture. Taking interest in their culture will make your students feel valued and important. This can help them feel that sense of belonging in the classroom. Moreover, different cultural days and religious holidays should be celebrated in the classroom to promote inclusion and harmony between students. Try to learn about their communities and their traditions. This not only creates a better classroom environment but an overall peaceful society. Moreover, this should not just apply to teachers. Everyone should try to learn about different cultures and partake in community events to create a stronger bond with these people.

Meet diverse learning needs

Not every student is the same and so they all have different rates and ways of learning. Some students can adapt pretty well to the concepts being taught in the class while others might need a practical demonstration. Some students are better in art subjects than science while others might prefer science subjects. The differences are countless. Having only one way of teaching is not the most beneficial way to help fulfill the diverse learning needs of students. You need to analyze what your students are good at doing and help them use these strengths in their own favor. Similarly identify their weaknesses and help them to overcome these weaknesses on their way to success. Try using technology when teaching your students. You may set up a camera in your classroom recording your lectures and then share that lecture with all students. This will help the students understand each concept better and rewatch the lectures anytime they want. As we all can agree, teaching is not one-size-fits-all. So, make sure to consider what works well in your classroom, re-evaluate things that are not improving the learning environment, and reflect on progress regularly.

Rearrange classroom seating to be inclusive of students with special needs

Classroom seating play a huge role in implementing an inclusive learning environment. It might not matter a lot in traditional classrooms in which most of the students can keep up with the pace of their curriculum and have relatively equal learning capabilities. However, when we shift to classrooms that are much more diverse, an inclusive seating arrangement becomes crucial. These days it is not a rare sight to watch classrooms filled with students from diverse backgrounds and cultures.

There is also a difference in the neurological and physical capabilities of each student since these classrooms also include special needs children. In such cases going by the traditional seating arrangement will not work. For example, students at the back of the classroom should be the ones having perfect eyesight and healthy hearing. Similarly, students at the front should be the ones who have trouble paying attention due to ADHD or have hearing loss. Letting your students sit randomly can disrupt the classroom equilibrium and inclusivity. You can look at the student profiles that you have in order to decide which seats they should sit on.

The below lesson plan offers a way to ensure inclusion within a classroom setting. The specific focus of this lesson is microaggressions, which is an important phenomenon to understand and address. Many of us may have behaviors that involve microaggressions without even realizing. But when we know better, we can act better—and do the same with our students.

Lesson plan: microaggressions

Lesson Topic: How to address Microaggressions and Build an Inclusive Classroom Culture.	
Lesson Aims: By the end of the lesson, learners will be better able to… • Understand the term Microaggression and discuss it • Create a more inclusive environment in the classroom	**Lesson Outcomes:** By the end of the lesson, learners will … • Know what Microaggressions are and the negative effects • Learn how to respond to microaggressions in a positive and effective manner
Anticipated difficulties: 1. Learners may not have retrospected on their classroom attitude 2. Learners might not be aware of the term Micro-aggression	**Suggested solutions:** 1. Ask them a few questions to look back at their behavior 2. Guide them about ways to stop microaggressions and promote acceptance in society

Stage name	Stage Aim	Teacher's Procedure
Warmer	To make the teachers think about the classroom issues and engage them in the lesson	Think about the following questions and write down answers based on your experiences: • Do you think that every student should be treated equally in a classroom? • Have you ever been in a class with students from different ethnicities? • Have you observed any change in behavior toward different students by other teachers or yourself? • Do you have a clear understanding of what microaggression is? After answering these questions, next phase is to understand the term micro-aggression.
Presentation	Enable the learners to understand the concept of microaggression and work on the ways to avoid it	**Understanding Microaggression in a classroom:** "Microaggressions are the everyday verbal, nonverbal, and environmental slights, snubs, or insults, whether intentional or unintentional, which communicate hostile, derogatory, or negative messages to target persons based solely upon their marginalized group membership. These hidden messages may invalidate the group

identity or experiential reality of target persons, demean them on a personal or group level, communicate they are lesser human beings, suggest they do not belong with the majority group, threaten and intimidate, or relegate them to inferior status and treatment. Microaggressions are active manifestations of our worldviews of inclusion/exclusion, superiority/inferiority, normality/abnormality, and desirability/undesirability."

Examples of Microaggression:

- We demonstrate surprise when a boy has good handwriting or prefers theater to sports, or when a girl is good at calculus and engineering.

- We don't try to pronounce a student's name correctly as it is from a culture with which we are not familiar. Instead, we decide to call him, "Sam," because it is just easier to remember.

It can be expressed in:

- Setting low expectations for students from particular groups or neighborhoods.

- Calling on and engaging one gender, class, or race of students while ignoring other students.

		<ul><li>Anticipating students' emotional responses based on gender, sexual orientation, race, or ethnicity.</li><li>Using inappropriate humor in class that degrades students from different groups.</li><li>Using the term "illegals" to reference undocumented students.</li><li>Denying the experiences of students by questioning the credibility and validity of their stories.</li><li>Using sexist language.</li></ul>Though we claim to be non-racist and unbiased, we can perpetuate diminishing, hurtful microaggressions and outright bias with and without meaning it. **Impact of Microaggression in classroom:**<ul><li>Leads to feelings of Isolation</li><li>Undermines credibility as an educator</li><li>Creates hostile learning environment</li></ul>**Dealing With Microaggression: Recognition**<ul><li>Recognize that a microaggression occurred.</li><li>Accept your feelings in the moment and reach out to someone you can talk to.</li></ul>

| | | • Take care of yourself. Talk things over with peers and practice healthy sleeping habits and self-care strategies, such as mindfulness. **Critical Reflection** • Take a step back and think about how you want to respond. Consider the context. What is your relationship with the person? Decide how you want to respond. • If possible, take the incident and turn it into a teaching/learning moment for the person who said the microaggression and the bystanders who did not address it. **Appropriate Action** Speak to the aggressor or ask a third party to do so if you feel uncomfortable and take action to protect yourself. Ask questions like: • "This/that makes me feel uncomfortable." • "May I give you some feedback?" • "I'd prefer you don't use language like that." • "I'm offended by that." • "I know you didn't intend this, but when you said _____, I |

		felt _____ because _____."
		• "I noticed you have difficulty pronouncing my name. Can I help?"
		If you cause a microaggression:
		Awareness
		• Engage in self-reflection.
		• Become aware of your own biases, anxieties, and motivations behind the harm.
		Acceptance
		• Take accountability for your actions.
		• Acknowledge the other person's hurt and apologize.
		• Move away from shame, denial, and embarrassment.
		Action
		• Educate yourself about your actions and take this as a learning experience to improve yourself.
		• Engage in critical thinking.
		• Seek help from others.
		• Make things right by listening to the harmed.
		• "Can you help me understand what just happened?"
		• "Thank you for letting me know how my comment made you feel. No one has ever brought this to my attention before. If you're willing to talk more about

		it, I'd like to better understand the ways my comment was problematic so I can learn from this and help educate others. However, I recognize that it is up to me to learn more – not for you to teach me."
		• "I want to make this right," you might say. "If you have the energy or time, please let me know if there's something I can do. I'd like to better understand the ways my comment was problematic so I can learn from this and help educate others. However, I recognize that it is up to me to learn more – not for you to teach me." Pairing this with a sincere apology and a recognition of the labor that was already done on your behalf definitely does not hurt.
		• "I'm sorry that what I said hurt you. That wasn't my intention, but I will be intentional about trying to avoid hurting others in that way in the future."

Production	Enables learners to reflect on their understanding and practice it by relating it to any incidence	**Reflection** Since you're more likely to give in to your biases when you're under pressure, practice ways to reduce stress and increase mindfulness, such as focused breathing. Pause and reflect to reduce reflexive actions. Think and write about an imaginary incidence where microaggression occurs in a class, how will you deal with it and what steps will you take to avoid it in future?
References		• Sue, D. W., Lin, A. I., Torino, G. C., Capodilupo, C. M., & Rivera, D. P. (2009). Racial microaggressions and difficult dialogues on race in the classroom. *Cultural Diversity and Ethnic Minority Psychology, 15*(2), 183-190. • Sue, D. W., Capodilupo, C. M., Torino, G. C., Bucceri, J. M., Holder, A. M., Nadal, K. L., et al. (2007). Racial microaggressions in everyday life: Implications for clinical practice. *American Psychologist, 62,* 271-286.

Conclusion

Becoming culturally aware is something we should all strive for. However, indulging too much into different cultures and not paying enough attention to your own cultural identity can have the opposite effect. When people leave their birthplace to settle abroad, they often start losing the sense of their personal identity. They start morphing into a new identity that is similar to the environment and people around them. This is just to get accepted into their new home. Of course, there is nothing wrong in changing or adapting but letting go of who you are just to get accepted is the wrong approach. Inclusion and the sense of belonging have to do with being yourself and still getting accepted. It allows people to be more tolerant towards others. The journey towards one's own cultural identity may cause them to appreciate other cultures too.

The main point of becoming culturally aware and inclusive is not to get rid of all differences and become a single identity. It is to appreciate those differences and still live as one. Our goal is to get to a point where the color of someone's skin does not decide how they are treated in society. How we treat people should only depend on their character and how they behave. Diversity is natural and there is nothing we can do to change it. What we can do is to live in harmony with each other and treat everyone how we would like to be treated. We need to teach our children that these factors do not determine a person's capabilities and talents. Teach them about incredible people like Stephen Hawking, Nelson Mandela, Malala Yousafzai and Mahatma Gandhi to make them realize that skin color, gender and physical attributes have nothing to do with achieving greatness.

I know there is still a long way to go before we can finally create a world where people are not seen as black or white but as humans. A world where immigrants are not told to go back to their own country, where people are treated as equals. We still have a lot to do and change but I'm sure that our future generations would be educated enough to eradicate discrimination and injustice based on social identity. When it comes to implementing a major change in society, it takes a lot of time. There are a lot of different reasons for this but one of the major ones is our preconceived beliefs. Adults have trouble changing their past beliefs as compared to children. That's why the younger generation is much more tolerant and accepting. These newer generations of people are much more used to differences and cultures, so they do not have much problem accepting them. So, one of the ways in which we can make a progressive and inclusive society is to expose our children to diversity and cultural awareness.

Imagine a person being locked up in a dark room. They are provided with enough food to survive but no outside contact. What will become of this person after 5 years if they keep living in that dark room? Of course, they would struggle to communicate and bond with other people. It is not because of hate or discrimination; it is just because of a lack of exposure. The same can happen to people who don't have much exposure to other cultures and people of varying ethnicities. Therefore, encouraging your children to have a diverse group of friends is important.

Different organizations have already realized the importance of having diversity in the workplace. It promotes productivity and creativity among people. Moreover, diversity is also linked to a much more competitive working environment. As people from divergent backgrounds get together, they put forward their own ideas and perspectives which collectively help the whole company to grow. However, a diverse workplace also requires inclusivity and belonging for its employees. The same is true for classrooms and even households.

But why even bother? Why would someone take their time off and try to understand different cultures? Why go out of your own way to promote inclusion and a sense of belonging. It is probably a matter of choice. Do you want to create a better future for your kids in which they can be free to do whatever they want (within the terms of law of course) and be whoever they want to be. A world where people will not discriminate against your child just because of how they look or how they think. A world where society is able to escape the chains of racial discrimination and hate. If your answer is yes, then start that journey of change today! Start with your children and act as a role model for them. Starting this journey at your own household may not seem like a big change but as Diana Cooper said:

"Change one small thing today and bigger changes will follow."

Final takeaways

o People are more tolerable of each other.

o There is still a long way to go before people completely become comfortable with each other and with different cultures.

o People are accepting diversity and it is becoming a necessity in many places.

o Equity, inclusion, and belonging are important.

o How will acceptance of cultural diversity, having equity in society, and a sense of inclusion and belonging help future generations? (How we need to teach these things to our children and first adopt ourselves so that our children have a better future)?

The Cultural Landscape

Recipes

As something that we all integrate in our daily lives, in a variety of ways, food reflects our habits, beliefs, upbringings, and cultures. On a bigger scale, it also reflects entire, or cross-cultural interaction. Take, for example, the prevalence of fusion cuisines or cuisines that have been adapted from their origin to cater to tastes of a different community.

Because of its essential nature, food is something we can appreciate, bond over, and share. However, strong feelings and identifications with foods can also cause or reflect conflict. In the American South, for example, barbeque sauce is a contentious subject; mustard-based sauces versus vinegar-based sauces can be a surprisingly heated topic. Jollof rice is another such subject. The West African dish is usually made with rice, tomatoes, onions, spices, vegetables, and meat, but ingredients and cooking methods vary from region to region. Recipes for Cameroonian jollof rice, which I grew up eating has been included as an example. There is certainly rivalry among West African communities about the best type of jollof rice.

Food can thus be a great way to explore and reflect upon culture, whether it is our own or from somewhere unfamiliar. This section of the book provides various recipes as a starting point for doing this in your own home. You can keep things simple and just try out a new dish to serve your family. You could also make it a more significant experience––perhaps choosing a new country or culture each month with your children and exploring it over the course of a few weeks. One week might involve cooking a meal typical in that area or community. You could even play music in the background as you cook together. You could also try finding a local restaurant that serves food from that culture and having a meal out together–– and supporting a small business at the same time. Following weeks could explore the culture in more depth, perhaps through watching a documentary or movie, visiting a museum with a relevant exhibit, learning a few words in a different language, attending an unfamiliar celebration or religious holiday…there are so many options! The best part is this book simply serves as a starting point, and you can proceed however you like.

Cameroonian Jollof Rice

This recipe was taken from YouTube user Seasoning Angels.

Ingredients

- 5 cups rice
- Vegetable oil
- 1lb beef or shrimp
- 1 cup chopped onion
- 3 cups chopped tomatoes
- 1 tbsp beef Maggi
- 1 tbsp garlic powder
- 1 tbsp salt
- White pepper
- Paprika
- Minced garlic
- 1 tbsp ginger paste
- Mixed vegetables, such as corn, beans, carrots

Instructions

1. Wash the rice.

2. Salt the beef and then fry until golden brown and crisp. Remove from frying pan then add tomatoes and onion to pan. Fry for several minutes, then add spices and stir together.

3. Add vegetables, stir.

4. Add the cooked beef.

5. Add 5 cups of washed rice and 1.5cups water for every 5 cups rice.

6. Add shrimp and pepper. Cover the pot and let simmer over low heat.

7. Once liquid is absorbed and rice is cooked, the dish is done.

Puerto Rico: Arroz Mamposteao, Red Beans and Rice

This recipe was submitted by Tanya Nyrka. Bayne. Her late mother, Aida Lydia Quiñones Márquez de Bayne, cooked this meal often while raising her family in The Bronx, New York.

Ingredients

- Arroz mamposteao/red rice
- 1 clove garlic, chopped
- 2 ounces Puerto Rican longaniza sausage
- 1 tablespoon sofrito
- 1 tablespoon fresh cilantro
- 4 cups cooked white rice
- 2 cups red bean stew
- 2 tablespoons fresh calabaza (or butternut squash)
- 1 tablespoon aioli (recipe follows)

Red bean stew

- 2 tablespoons olive oil
- 1½ teaspoons garlic

- 1 onion
- 2 tablepoons sofrito
- 1 tablespoon recaito sauce
- 2 bay leaves
- 1/2 cup tomato sauce
- 1 packet sazón seasoning
- 1 tablespoon fresh cilantro
- 2 15.5-ounce cans of large red beans

Aioli

- 3 garlic cloves
- ¼ teaspoon salt
- 1 cup mayonnaise
- 2 teaspoons fresh lemon juice
- White pepper

Preparation

For red bean stew:

1. In a sauce pot, at medium high heat, sauté the garlic and white onions in the olive oil until translucent.
2. Add the sofrito and recaito and cook for an additional minute.

3. Add the bay leaves, tomato sauce, seasoning packet, chopped cilantro and beans and stir together to incorporate well.

4. Bring to a boil, reduce temperature to low and continue cooking for about 30 minutes.

For aioli:

1. Mince the garlic with salt in small bowl to form a smooth paste.

2. Whisk in the mayonnaise and the lemon juice.

3. Season to taste with salt and white pepper.

For arroz mamposteao:

1. In a large skillet, at medium high temperature, sauté garlic until toasted in the olive oil. Add the sliced longaniza sausage, sofrito and chopped cilantro and cook for about a minute and a half.

2. Add the cooked rice and combine well.

3. Slowly and gently stir in the bean stew, being careful not to smash the beans. Also, calabaza or butternut squash, and stir until the ingredients are well incorporated. Garnish with fresh cilantro and drizzle with aioli.

Jerk Chicken

This recipe was taken from Nomnomeverywhere, a blog dedicated to international cuisine (https://nomnomeverywhere.wordpress.com/2013/06/27/food-next-door-you-cook-i-eat-fufu-watercress-jerk-chicken/).

Ingredients

- Chicken (a whole large fowl, about 4-5 lbs.)
- 1 large onion (chopped or sliced into crescents)
- 5-7 cloves of garlic (chopped or ground)
- Equal parts ginger as garlic (ground)
- ½ tsp. of salt
- 3-4 small cubes of Maggi (1-2 bouillon cubes)
- 1-2 tsp. black pepper
- 1-2 tsp. seasoned meat tenderizer (5th Season)
- 1-2 tsp. Adobo All Purpose Seasoning with Cumin (Goya)
- 4-5 tbsp. Jamaican Jerk Seasoning
- ¼ – ½ cup vegetable oil
- Optional: 1 habanero pepper

For Jerk Chicken (the easiest!)

1. If your chicken was not pre-carved, hack it away into the familiar cuts i.e., drumsticks, thighs, breast, etc.

2. Place chicken in pot and mix in all ingredients. Yes, ALL of them. Start gently with the salt and Maggi. Add a bit of water (about 1/2 cup) to get a boil going. Tip: Normally, fresh chicken in the U.S. comes plumped with quite a bit of fluid so you don't need to add water. The chicken just exudes these fluids as it cooks. However, if unsure, always start out with just a bit of water and monitor closely. You can always manually reduce the liquid or let it boil away to your comfort level.

3. As the chicken mix starts boiling/cooking, periodically taste the juices for salt/spice level (every 10 mins at least). Gently augment Maggi/spices and water as needed.

4. Let the chicken cook for at least 25-30 mins. Stir and flip pieces as needed, to expose them to more heat.

5. When chicken is done (liquid level should be super low, if any is left at all), turn off the heat. All done!

Madhur Jaffrey's Chicken Korma

Madhur Jaffrey is an Indian-British-American actress and food writer, a well-known voice in food writing. This recipe, taken from BBC Food, is for chicken korma which is best served with rice and a drop of cream right before serving. Due to Britain's history of empire and colonization, Indian food is extremely popular throughout the country, and curry is easy to find. Reflecting on the presence of different cuisines in a region can reveal insights about history, immigration, and cross-cultural interactions.

Ingredients

- 5-6 garlic cloves, coarsely chopped
- 2.5cm/1in piece fresh root ginger, chopped
- 50g/2oz flaked almonds
- 150ml/¼ pint water
- 5 tbsp olive or groundnut oil
- 2 bay leaves
- 8 cardamom pods, lightly crushed
- 4 cloves
- 2.5cm/1in piece cinnamon stick

- 1 onion, finely chopped
- 1 tbsp ground cumin
- 1 tbsp ground coriander
- ¼ tsp chili powder
- 1 tbsp tomato purée
- 1¼ tsp salt
- ½ tbsp garam masala
- 3 tbsp double cream
- 1.5kg/3lb chicken pieces, skinned and cut into serving portions (breast cut in half across the center)

Method

1. Put the garlic, ginger and almonds into the bowl of a food processor.
2. Turn on the food processor and pour six tablespoons of the water through the funnel and blend to a smooth paste (if your food processor does not have a funnel, just add the water before blending).
3. Heat the oil in a wide pan set over a high heat. When it is very hot, add the bay leaves, cardamom pods, cloves and cinnamon stick and stir for ten seconds (take care because they may spit when they hit the oil).

4. Add the onion and cook for several minutes, stirring, until it is a medium brown color. Reduce the heat to medium-high once the onion begins to brown.

5. Add the paste from the food processor and stir. Cook, stirring, for 3-4 minutes or until lightly browned.

6. Add the cumin, coriander and chili powder and cook, stirring, for 30 seconds. Add the tomato puree and stir for a minute longer.

7. Add the salt, garam masala, cream and remaining water and stir together.

8. Add the chicken pieces and stir to coat them with the spice paste.

9. Bring to a simmer, then cover the pan, turn the heat to low and simmer gently for 25 minutes, or until the chicken is cooked through, turning the chicken pieces over several times during cooking.

10. Transfer to a serving dish and serve with your choice of Indian breads and chutneys, rice, or vegetables.

Khati Khati & Fufu Corn

This dish is typical of where I grew up—my beloved tribe Nso, in the Northwest region of Cameroon in Central West Africa. It is suggested to serve khati khati with greens of your choice, corn fufu, oatmeal fufu, or steamed rice. The khati khati recipe is from "The Motherland Cookbook: Easy, Tasty, Healthy but not fast" by Sabina Leyla Jules.

Ingredients

- 1 Chicken (preferably whole, free-range chicken)
- 2 cups palm oil
- 1 large onion
- 2 roma (plum) tomatoes
- 2 teaspoons of Mammy Doro Chicken Seasoning
- 1 teaspoon Mammy Doro African Blue Basil (masepo/nchanwu)
- Salt, Maggi, Knorr, or Bouillon cubes to taste.

Instructions

1. Cut up the chicken into 4 parts, marinate with salt and Maggi, Knorr, or Bouillon cubes.

2. Place chicken on the grill (do not remove skin; fat melts during grilling and shields chicken from drying up and burning). After grilling chicken (half cooked), cut into bite sizes, and put in a large saucepan.

3. Blend onion and tomatoes. Add to the chicken, along with 5 cups water or as needed to cook the chicken. Do not add too much water.

4. Add 2 cups of palm oil, 1 teaspoon of MammyDoro African Basil, and 2 teaspoons of MammyDoro Chicken Seasoning. Add salt and Maggi to taste and cook until chicken is tender.

Fufu Corn

Ingredients

- 2 cups white/yellow corn meal
- 5 cups of water
- foil or saran wrap

Instructions

1. Bring 2½ cups of water to a gentle simmer in a medium sauce pot. In a separate bowl, mix 2 cups of cornmeal with about 2 cups of room temp water. Carefully add into simmering water. Reduce heat to medium and use a strong wooden spoon to stir occasionally. Cook for about 7 minutes; it will thicken. Then add in 1/3 cup of warm water, cover and cook for another 5-7 minutes. Use dominant hand and mix thoroughly, breaking any chunks until smooth.

2. Cut saran wrap or foil paper big enough to wrap fufu corn. Place on chopping board or flat surface. Set aside a bowl with warm water. Dip ladle in water (prevents sticking), then scoop dough or fufu

unto saran wrap. Carefully raise edges into a bundle, twist 1-2 times and place on a plate twist side down. Repeat until all dough is used. Let cool for a few minutes to solidify. Unwrap and serve with kati kati and Njama Njama

Greetings in Different Languages

Learning vocabulary in a new language can also be a fun way to incorporate intercultural education in an easy and non-intimidating way. Try using some of the examples below. When looking at them with your children, find videos online of native speakers saying the word aloud. Doing this provides more accurate examples, and it can also spark further discussions with your children. They may also be intrigued by different alphabets, and you can even find resources online for learning characters in Mandarin, for example.

The table below includes a very small selection of our world's spoken languages. Several languages from Africa are included––it is a huge continent consisting of 54 fully recognized countries, each with its own ethnic groups, languages, cultures, and traditions. In Cameroon, for example, there are over 250 tribes and three major ethnic groups: the Bantus, semi-Bantus, and Sudanese. While the country's official or most common languages for communication are English and French, the number of dialects and languages present within the country is over 260. Some languages, including a couple below, do not have direct translations for "good morning" or "good evening."

Discussing topics such as this can be a helpful reminder of the diversity that surrounds us, whether nearby or far from us.

Tribe/Country	Language	*"Hello"*	*"Good morning"*	*"Good evening"*
1. Nso (Cameroon)	Lamnso	N/A	Yi ran ni wo	Yi ji nia
2. Spain	Spanish	Hola	Buenos días	Buenas noches
3. France	French	Salut	Bonjour	Bonsoir
4. Bali (Cameroon)	Mughaka	N/A	Ou lah ndi	N/A
5. Igbo (Nigeria)	Igbo	Nnọọ	ụtụtụ ọma	mgbede ọma
6. Yoruba (Nigeria)	Yoruba	Pẹlẹ o	e kaaro	ka a ale
7. India	Hindi	Namaste	Suprabhaat	Shubh sundhya a

8. **Turkey**	Turkish	Merhaba / Selam	Günaydı	iyi akşamlar
9. **Japan**	Japanese	こんにちわ Kon-nichiwa	おはようございます Ohayō gozai-masu	こんばんわ Kon-banwa
10. **Jamaica**	Pat-ois/patoire	Blessings	Gud Mawn-ing	Gud Evening
11. **Ghana**	Akan twi	Agoo	Me ma wo akye	Me ma wo adwo
12. **Korea**	Korean	안녕하세요 annyeong haseyo	좋은아침이에요 (joeun achimieyo)	N/A
13. **China**	Mandarin	你好 Nǐ hǎo	下午好 Xiàwǔ hǎo	晚安 Wǎn'ān

Reading Guide for Parents & Educators

The following questions and discussion topics are intended to provide inspiration, structure, and guidance as you reflect on cultural identity. Some questions are geared towards parents and educators, and some can be used to foster open dialogues with your children.

Chapter 1: Culture and Society

- Did studying interactions across cross cultures give us hope to better our relations with our children?

- How do we plan on understanding our culture and religion better to be able to accept opposing ones around us?

- Did you make a list of the questions you wish to introduce at the dinner table?

- What boundaries do we wish to teach our children in helping them create balances between preserving their own identity as well as appreciating the others'?

- How can we escape the traditional model of the family and go beyond assigned gender roles for a more effective primary socialization for our children?

Chapter 2: The Power of Cultural Identity

- Make a list of the days in a week you are free and try to set parent-teacher meetings to get to know your child better in a classroom setting, which could be very different to how they are at home.

- How can you stay on friendly terms with the kids? Give them the space to culturally explore themselves but also provide them the safe space to discuss it with you. Staying stern with them always and conditioning them to stay a certain way distance them even more.

- As a teacher, try to set up individual meetings with the children to find ways in bettering the curriculum based on their experiences and your shortcomings.

- How can you get to know your students? Start early in the school year and set an example by introducing yourself, then encourage them do the same––explain where they come from, what they like and dislike, and share something about their culture. Take special note of how students spell and pronounce their names.

- Help younger kids devise and discipline their timetables to maintain a balance between their daily interactions, so that they do not get biased views of who they wish to become. Exposure is vital.

Chapter 3: Sarah, a case study for identity

- Have you adjusted your identity to fit in with others? Think of examples.

- Have you strengthened parts of your identity at times? Think of examples.

- If you have adjusted your identity, either to fit in or to stand out, why did you do so? How did it make you feel?

- Did you consider equity (unequal but fair distribution of resources on the basis of need) to seem unjust at first? What is your perspective on it now, and why did you think it changed?

Chapter 4: Why diversity matters

- As teachers, what are some of the ways you have devised that would help enhance your kids' knowledge over worldwide cultures and linguistics? Consider setting up a cultural society which gets run by the students themselves, with a perk of hosting and organizing an annual culture day as an incentive for inter-ethnic students to work together.

- Asking Gen Z students their take on how a hierarchy or power affects their cultural interactions within the classroom, i.e., any fears/hesitation.

- Illustrating real-life examples for kids to resolve misconceptions of the world around them which they desperately might be trying to comprehend.

Chapter 5: Modern-day culture, diversity, and identity

- How do we make sense of the globalized world of today?

- Have you constituted ways to help individuals understand identities better in a safe place without having to worry about a crisis of a sense of self?

- What conclusion do we draw from the link and balance between cultural homogenization and heterogenization?

- Do we intend to make our workplaces and classrooms more culturally intelligent and sensitive? If so, then what are some of the ways we can make this happen?

Chapter 6: Equity and equality

- How do we understand 'single stories', and why do we feel there is a need to find a 'balance of stories' to replace it?

- Do you think it is fair to blame the teachers, or a healthier approach would be best to investigate the organizational backing of the system?

- Adichie mentioned feeling guilty for treating others the same way she had been treated. Why do you think humans repeat each other's mistakes, and how can we help ourselves come out of cultural biases?

- Out of the many ways to establish equity within society, what measures did you find most effective?

- Did you consider equity (unequal but fair distribution of resources on the basis of need) to seem unjust at first? What is your perspective on it now, and why did you think it changed?

Chapter 7: Inclusion and identity

- What are some examples of diversity and inclusion protocol?

- Does your workplace or place of education currently have diversity and inclusion protocol in place for hiring or acceptance procedures? If so, what are they and have they been effective?

- Have you ever felt excluded because of your identity? How did you handle the situation? Providing anecdotes and examples to your children can be helpful in discussions.

- When have you benefited from power and privilege? Were you aware of it at the time?

- How can you use your power and privilege, whether related to your gender, race, age, nationality, ability, etc., to advocate for those who have less privilege than you do?

Chapter 8: Why inclusion matters

- How can seating arrangements be changed to create an inclusive environment in your own classroom?

- Can you think of any other effective plans to create inclusion in the classroom?

Chapter 9: Inclusion, a case study in education

- Is there a child or young person in your life who has a disability of some sort? What has their process been for pursuing accommodations at school?

- Are there ways that you can better accommodate students' abilities in the classroom?

- How can you support parents who have a child with a disability? How can you communicate and express your support to them?

Chapter 10: When the magic happens

- How can you best meet your child or students' needs? What can you do to familiarize yourself with their disability or learning difference and advocate for them in the classroom?

- Who do you want to advocate for your child at school? Having a number of trustworthy advocates that you communicate with regularly can ensure an effective support system.

- What can you do to advocate for your student and ensure their needs are met?

- How can you show your student how to advocate for themselves? Are there resources in the community that can help you and your student understand how they learn best?

- What brings you hope in your journey alongside your student? What brings you fear or frustration? Identifying positive and negative influences can give you motivation in difficult times, as well as areas for continued improvement or monitoring.

Chapter 11: Guide for parents

- How do you balance integrating your family and staying true to your roots?

- How do you keep your culture alive in your family? How do you keep your culture or traditions active?

Chapter 12: Guide for educators

- What was a successful learning moment in your classroom?

- What made you realize you need to be more inclusive in your classroom?

- What is an example of a successful activity or conversation about culture, diversity, etc. in your classroom?

About the Author

Dr. Eunice Gwanmesia, PhD, MSN, MSHCA, RN

Eunice Gwanmesia is an award-winning thought leader with more than 20 years of success as a registered nurse (RN), professor, and diversity, equity, and inclusion (DE&I) advocate. A prolific author and speaker who made her way across the globe from Cameroon to the United States, Dr. Gwanmesia engages audiences in the classroom, workplace, and around the world in conversations about diversity, cultural differences, and how to use them to improve organizational performance. She possesses master's degrees in Nursing and Healthcare Administration, a Ph.D. in Nursing, a professional coaching certification, and several DE&I-related certificates. She worked as an RN in various medical centers, taught nursing for 13 years at Delaware State University, and graduated 200+ Certified Nursing Assistants from Always Health Care

Services, a trade school she established. In 2017, Dr. Gwanmesia founded Eunity Solutions to help organizations maximize human capital through cultural awareness and the appreciation of differences. She founded and leads the Caregiver Support Foundation, serves on various committees with organizations like the Delaware African Caribbean Affairs Commission, and is highly active in her community.

HIRE DR. EUNICE TO SPEAK AT YOUR EVENT
OR FACILITATE WORKSHOPS IN YOUR
SCHOOL DISTRICT OR ORGANIZATION

www.dreunicespeaks.com/keynote

www.eunitysolutions.com

References

Adichie, C. N. (2012). *The Danger of a Single Story* [Video]. Retrieved from TED Conferences: https://www.ted.com/talks/chimamanda_ngozi_adichie_the_d anger_of_a_single_story

Anti-Defamation League. (2018). *Pyramid of Hate.* Retrieved from Anti-Defamation League: https://www.adl.org/sites/default/files/documents/pyramid-of-hate.pdf

Beck, U. (2006). *Cosmopolitan Vision.* Polity.

Benner, A., & Graham, S. (2013). The antecedents and consequences of racial/ethnic discrimination during adolescence: Does the source of discrimination matter? *Developmental Psychology, 49*(8), 1602-1613.

Berry, J., & Sabatier, C. (2011). Variations in the assessment of acculturation attitudes: Their relationships with psychological wellbeing. *International Journal of Intercultural Relations*, 658-669.

Carter, P. (2006). Straddling Boundaries: Identity, Culture, and School. *Sociology of Education.*

Cuff, E., Dennis, A., Francis, D., & Sharrock, W. (2016). *Perspectives in Sociology* (Vol. 5). Routledge.

Dass, M., & Vinnakota, S. (2019). Cross-Cultural Mistakes by Renowned Brands - Evaluating the Success and Failures of Brands in Host Nations. *International Journal of Trend in Scientific Research and Development, 3*(2), 38-43.

Dictionary.com. (2020, November 4). *What Is The Difference Between "Equality" And "Equity"?* Retrieved 2022, from https://www.dictionary.com/e/equality-vs-equity/

DiFranza, A. (2019, June 24). *4 Practices to Promote Equity in the Classroom.* Retrieved from Northeastern University: https://www.northeastern.edu/graduate/blog/equity-in-the-classroom/

Durkheim, É. (1956). *Education and Sociology.* Simon and Schuster.

Güneri, O., Sümer, Z., & Yildirim, A. (1999). Sources of self-identity among Turkish adolescents. *Adolescence, 34*(135), 535-546.

George Ritzer. (1993). *The McDonaldization of society.* Newbury Park: Pine Forge Press.

Hall, E. (1976). *Beyond Culture.* Knopf Doubleday Publishing Group.

Hofstede, G. (1984). Cultural dimensions in management and planning. *Asia Pacific Journal of Management,* 81-99.

Hughes, J., Cavell, T., & Wilson, V. (2001). Further Support for the Developmental Significance of the Quality of the Teacher–Student Relationship. *Journal of School Psychology, 39*(4), 289-301.

Identity and Belonging - Mind metaphors: English and Psychology collide. (n.d.). Retrieved August 27, 2022, from Mind metaphors: English and Psychology collide: https://mindmetaphors.weebly.com/identity–and–belonging.html

Iqbal, M. (n.d.). *Elders on Campus*. (Ryerson School of Journalism) Retrieved 2022, from Indigenous Land Urban Studies: https://indigenouslandurbanstories.ca/portfolio–item/elders–on–campus/

Jennings, J. (2011). *Globalizations and the Ancient World.* Cambridge University Press.

Linton, R. (2013). *The cultural background of personality.* Routledge.

Liu, Y. (2012). Exploring the Impacts of Cultural Globalization on Cultural Awareness/ Values and English Writing in Chinese Context. *Intercultural Communication Studies*, 94-110.

Mind Metaphors. (n.d, n.d n.d). *Exploring Identity and Belonging*. Retrieved from Mind Metaphors: English and Psychology: https://mindmetaphors.weebly.com/identity–and–belonging.html#:~:text=Our%20relationships%20help%20strengthen%20our,in%20our%20sense%20of%20belonging.

Parker, K., Graf, N., & Igielnik, R. (2019). *Generation Z Looks a Lot Like Millenials on Key Social and Political Issues.* Pew Research Center.

Shinde, N. (2017). The Beginning of Inclusion – Classroom Seating Discipline. *Learning Curve*, 5-6.

Stadler-Heer S. (2019). *Inclusion.* (ELT Journal.;73(2):219-222. ed.). Retrieved from doi:10.1093/elt/ccz004

Stevens, W. (2021). Blackfishing on Instagram: Influencing and the Commodification of Black Urban Aesthetics. *Social Media + Society,* 7(3).

Study Smarter. (n.d.). *Consumption Identity.* Retrieved from Study Smarter: https://www.studysmarter.co.uk/explanations/social-studies/cultural-identity/consumption-identity/

Thijs, J. (2017). Student–Teacher Relationships and Inter-ethnic Relations. In A. Rutland, D. Nesdale, & C. Brown, *The Wiley Handbook of Group Processes in Children and Adolescents.* John Wiley and Sons.

Thomas, D., & Creary, S. (2012). *Shifting the Diversity Climate: The Sodexo Solution.* Harvard Business School.

van Ameijde, J., & Weller, M. (2015). Designing for Student Retention. *Education,* 180-204.

Wright, C. (1992). *Race Relations in the Primary School* (Vol. 1997). David Fulton Publishers.

www.ingramcontent.com/pod-product-compliance
Lightning Source LLC
Chambersburg PA
CBHW062124020426
42335CB00013B/1086